THE NEW PR TOOLKIT

Strategies for Successful
Media Relations

Deirdre Breakenridge
Thomas J. DeLoughry

ISBN 0-13-009025-5

92495

9 790130 090255

THE NEW PR TOOLKIT

Strategies for Successful Media Relations

Deirdre Breakenridge
Thomas J. DeLoughry

FT Prentice Hall
FINANCIAL TIMES

An Imprint of PEARSON EDUCATION
Upper Saddle River, NJ • New York • London • San Francisco • Toronto • Sydney
Tokyo • Singapore • Hong Kong • Cape Town • Madrid
Paris • Milan • Munich • Amsterdam

www.ft-ph.com

A CIP catalogue record for this book can be obtained from the Library of Congress.

Production Editor and Compositor: *Vanessa Moore*
Executive Editor: *Jim Boyd*
Full-Service Production Manager: *Anne R. Garcia*
Marketing Manager: *John Pierce*
Manufacturing Buyer: *Maura Zaldivar*
Manfacturing Manager: *Alexis R. Heydt*
Cover Design Director: *Jerry Votta*
Cover Design: *Talar Boorujy*
Interior Design: *Gail Cocker-Bogusz*

 © 2003 Pearson Education, Inc.
Publishing as Financial Times Prentice Hall
Upper Saddle River, NJ 07458

Prentice Hall books are widely used by corporations and government agencies for training, marketing, and resale.

For information regarding corporate and government bulk discounts, please contact: Corporate and Government Sales (800) 382-3419 or corpsales@pearsontechgroup.com

Company and product names mentioned herein are the trademarks or registered trademarks of their respective owners.

Printed in the United States of America
10 9 8 7 6 5 4 3 2 1

ISBN 0-13-009025-5

Pearson Education LTD.
Pearson Education Australia PTY, Limited
Pearson Education Singapore, Pte. Ltd.
Pearson Education North Asia Ltd.
Pearson Education Canada, Ltd.
Pearson Educación de Mexico, S.A. de C.V.
Pearson Education—Japan
Pearson Education Malaysia, Pte. Ltd.

FINANCIAL TIMES PRENTICE HALL BOOKS

For more information, please go to www.ft-ph.com

Dr. Judith M. Bardwick
   Seeking the Calm in the Storm: Managing Chaos in Your Business Life
Gerald R. Baron
   Now Is Too Late: Survival in an Era of Instant News
Thomas L. Barton, William G. Shenkir, and Paul L. Walker
   Making Enterprise Risk Management Pay Off: How Leading Companies Implement Risk Management
Michael Basch
   CustomerCulture: How FedEx and Other Great Companies Put the Customer First Every Day
J. Stewart Black and Hal B. Gregersen
   Leading Strategic Change: Breaking Through the Brain Barrier
Deirdre Breakenridge
   Cyberbranding: Brand Building in the Digital Economy
Deirdre Breakenridge and Thomas J. DeLoughry
   The New PR Toolkit: Strategies for Successful Media Relations
William C. Byham, Audrey B. Smith, and Matthew J. Paese
   Grow Your Own Leaders: How to Identify, Develop, and Retain Leadership Talent
Jonathan Cagan and Craig M. Vogel
   Creating Breakthrough Products: Innovation from Product Planning to Program Approval
David M. Carter and Darren Rovell
   On the Ball: What You Can Learn About Business from Sports Leaders
Subir Chowdhury
   Organization 21C: Someday All Organizations Will Lead this Way
Subir Chowdhury
   The Talent Era: Achieving a High Return on Talent
Sherry Cooper
   Ride the Wave: Taking Control in a Turbulent Financial Age
James W. Cortada
   21st Century Business: Managing and Working in the New Digital Economy
James W. Cortada
   Making the Information Society: Experience, Consequences, and Possibilities
Aswath Damodaran
   The Dark Side of Valuation: Valuing Old Tech, New Tech, and New Economy Companies
Henry A. Davis and William W. Sihler
   Financial Turnarounds: Preserving Enterprise Value
Ross Dawson
   Living Networks: Leading Your Company, Customers, and Partners in the Hyper-connected Economy
Jim Despain and Jane Bodman Converse
   And Dignity for All: Unlocking Greatness through Values-Based Leadership

To Jeff, Megan, Mom, Dad, Bill, and Jay:
Thank you for the love and support
in helping me to achieve my goals.
To my partners Jason and Dennis:
Thank you for making PFS
the incredible experience that it is!
— D. B.

With love and thanks to Maria, Ryan, and Kevin.
— T. J. D.

About Prentice Hall Professional Technical Reference

With origins reaching back to the industry's first computer science publishing program in the 1960s, and formally launched as its own imprint in 1986, Prentice Hall Professional Technical Reference (PH PTR) has developed into the leading provider of technical books in the world today. Our editors now publish over 200 books annually, authored by leaders in the fields of computing, engineering, and business.

Our roots are firmly planted in the soil that gave rise to the technical revolution. Our bookshelf contains many of the industry's computing and engineering classics: Kernighan and Ritchie's *C Programming Language*, Nemeth's *UNIX System Adminstration Handbook*, Horstmann's *Core Java*, and Johnson's *High-Speed Digital Design*.

PH PTR acknowledges its auspicious beginnings while it looks to the future for inspiration. We continue to evolve and break new ground in publishing by providing today's professionals with tomorrow's solutions.

PRENTICE
HALL
PTR

Contents

CHAPTER 9   WEBCASTS ARE WORTH
A SECOND TRY   123

PART III   PROTECTING THE BRAND   145

CHAPTER 10   MONITORING BRAND
COMMUNICATION   147

CHAPTER 15 LOOKING AHEAD   221

ACKNOWLEDGMENTS

It took approximately one full year to develop the contents of our book, *The New PR Toolkit*. If it weren't for the many professionals who assisted us throughout the process, it would have taken much longer. Many of the editors/journalists who contributed to this book were on deadline themselves, yet still managed to successfully meet our time requirements. We thank them wholeheartedly for that. We also want to thank the executives who took the time to provide us with candid input from their own personal accounts and experiences with respect to public relations and its growth on the Internet. This input not only supported our research, but also gave this book an honest look at the daily life of PR people and how they approach the Internet.

There are many people behind the scenes who stuck with us through this long process. We're thankful for our reviewers and developers, Russ, Tanya, and Jon, for helping us to mold *The New PR Toolkit*. We appreciate the many hours you spent reading and providing us with your welcomed comments, which guided us every step of the way.

Deirdre's special acknowledgments go to her partners at PFS Marketwyse, Jason Miletsky and Dennis Chominsky. Their tireless efforts to build PFS (24/7) provided us with many of the experiences recorded in our book. We thank them for the support and the fun along the way. Also a special thanks to Deirdre's staff for pitching in to give constant commentary and graphical elements for the book.

Tom would like to acknowledge his friends and colleagues in journalism, many of whom are not always big fans of the public relations industry, but still took the time to give their honest assessments of how the profession is using the new Internet tools.

Introduction

There's no denying that the Internet has been one of the most overly hyped technologies in human history. Newspapers, TV shows, magazines, and yes, even a few books promised us a revolutionary new business world in which hard-charging dot-coms stole markets away from established brick-and-mortar companies that were supposedly too stupid and slow moving to realize what was happening around them. All Americans would soon have personal Web pages and spend countless hours in online "communities" swapping advice with like-minded peers. Of course, that's only if they weren't running to the front door to accept deliveries of the books, toys, pet food, and sofas they bought online at low, low prices. Anyone who didn't recognize the magnitude of this Internet revolution and invest a few bucks in skyrocketing Internet stocks just didn't get it.

Today we know that the Internet mania of the late 1990s was as much about greed as it was about innovation. Investors, sold on the notion of a worldwide network of billions of consumers, bet on startups and pushed them to run hard despite poorly formed business plans, faulty technology, and total ignorance about the difficulty of cost-effectively delivering things like groceries or bedroom sets across wide geographic regions.

All has not been lost in the dot-com bust, however. The world has embraced this new medium of communication and it is not going to let go. The Internet might not be the megamarket previously advertised, but it has very quickly changed the way that business is done in nearly every industry—from finance to manufacturing, from real estate to retail, and most certainly in public relations.

Indeed, it is not hyperbole to argue that the field of public relations has been revolutionized. PR professionals schooled in the old world of pretty press kits and faxed press releases have had to adapt quickly. Overnight mail is no longer fast enough. Reporters, feeling the Internet's demands for immediacy, want instant access to press releases and updated versions of corporate fact sheets, executive backgrounders, and every kind of data that PR people can make available. They expect to find the information in online newsrooms, where all these items are located in one place.

Even more revolutionary, perhaps, is the fact that public relations people are increasingly finding themselves interacting with the public. Reporters and analysts are only one part of the job. The Internet has given customers, stockholders, prospective business partners, and others access to the materials developed by PR people. It is both a marvelous opportunity to get a client's message out to the public without the interference of reporters and a dangerously out-of-control situation in which facts, rumor, and innuendo can be circulated about a company in seriously damaging ways often under the radar of clipping and monitoring services employed to report on what's being said about a company in the press. The infamous Internet grapevine has already created big headaches for some of the country's most popular brands. From Heinz ketchup to Coors beer and even talk show hosts, such as Oprah Winfrey, no one can escape the Internet's ability to spread rumors like wildfire.

PR people obviously have not been hiding with their heads in the sand. Most are getting press releases out quickly via broadcast e-mail and many have invested countless hours in developing online pressrooms. But who is using these tools to greatest effect? What have they learned that others in PR should emulate? What have they learned that the rest of us should avoid? What potentially helpful new tools are on the horizon? How do companies keep their online PR strategies in line with what they're doing in the offline arena?

Our goal for this book is to answer these key questions for public relations professionals—regardless of whether their clients are new Internet companies or old manufacturers. Deirdre Breakenridge's first book, *Cyberbranding* (Prentice Hall, 2001), told marketers how to use the Internet to build their brands. Strong public relations was an element to that story, but *The New PR Toolkit* focuses intently on public relations to offer solid advice to practitioners. Despite this focus, we believe that marketing professionals, senior level decision makers, and entrepreneurs are sure to find value in the tips and case studies presented here.

We understand that the Internet fundamentally has changed PR; however, we also counsel a strong back-to-basics approach to avoid many of the pitfalls of unsuccessful strategies of recent years. Business is still business, even if there's an *e* hung on the front of it. Research and planning were often the enemies of dot-com executives living on souped-up "Internet time," but both functions are actually more important than ever as PR people struggle to determine who is interacting with their brands online and offline and how can they be presented with the best possible image of the company.

The New PR Toolkit is full of solid examples of companies that have used the Internet to improve their public relations efforts and of lessons that can be learned by some high-profile failures. Our "Odd Couple" authoring partnership (we won't identify who's Felix and who's Oscar) guarantees that readers get not only the perspectives of a PR professional who's represented clients such as JVC, GMAI, and Derek Jeter's Turn 2 Foundation, but also the views of an experienced editor who has fielded thousands of pitches and written hundreds of articles in his 15 years with respected publications such as *Internet World* and *The Chronicle of Higher Education*. PR people and reporters, whether they want to admit it or not, are partners in bringing information to readers and viewers. Our intent with this book is to point out successful strategies and tactics as seen through the eyes of the PR people who orchestrated them and the journalists who responded to them and gave the stories ink, airtime, or online play.

The first part of *The New PR Toolkit* helps you to lay the groundwork for your online PR efforts, explaining the importance of identifying your target audience and understanding its needs and wants. The short lives of several dot-coms help us point up the dangers of overlooking the importance of such research. Research results, we argue, must not be derived from secondary sources, but should come from primary, qualitative, and quantitative studies focused on the perceptions and well-being of a brand.

We tell you, the readers, about the tools available to you, running the gamut from online databases, tracking software, monitoring and clipping services, and so on, and use case studies to explain how they've been employed successfully.

The middle part of *The New PR Toolkit* is devoted to explaining how the news media have evolved in the Internet era and the tools that can be used to reach them. Journalists of the 21st Century are more deadline conscious than ever, as weekly publications produce nightly electronic newsletters, and daily newspapers publish twice-daily Web updates. The historically hard-charging wire services now get their stories to the online public within minutes of their writing. The demands on their time and the power of the Internet means that many journalists consider faxes and overnight mail to be akin to the Pony Express. They want instant access to information through your Web site or via e-mail, but the details they want are the same as what they've been seeking for years. They want exclusives. They want to know in a timely fashion about big-money deals and industry-altering product announcements. They still love colorful personalities, preferably in conflict with equally colorful rivals. Getting personal access to such bigwigs is still tremendously important to most journalists and a task still best handled by PR professionals in the flesh, rather than their Internet-based tools.

We offer specific advice and case studies to illustrate exactly how to construct effective pitches in e-mail, complete with compelling subject lines. We discuss the use of permission-based e-mail that can keep reporters updated on your company while protecting you from being branded with the odious and possibly debilitating label of spammer. We discuss the essential elements of an online newsroom and offer our advice on how to produce an effective and accessible Webcast to get your executives out in front of the worldwide press.

In the final part of *The New PR Toolkit*, we focus on the pieces of a solid online public relations strategy that extend beyond day-to-day interactions with reporters or the public. We note, for example, the incredible speed of Internet communications and the importance of protecting your company from the damaging effects of message boards and rogue Web sites that spread less-than-pleasant words about your brand. As dissatisfied online users bad-mouth brands (you know the rule: have a good experience and you're likely to tell three people, have a bad experience and you tell 50 people), reporters often stumble across these postings and some might receive wider press coverage unless the affected company has a way of monitoring and intervening to protect its name.

Another important element of an online strategy must be a crisis management capability that lets a company get information out quickly on any number of newsmaking events from plane crashes to oil spills to product recalls. The Internet audience expects to be able to go to a company's site for the latest news, which means that PR professionals need to have a ghost template ready to go live, one that is developed before a crisis occurs and can be quickly updated with the latest details and posted to the Web site. A quick online response of the type employed on September 11, 2001, by companies such as United Airlines and Sandler O'Neill & Partners can make a company appear proactive rather than defensive and can be supplemented later with materials such as written statements, legal documents, or video of the CEO's remarks that give the company's story in full.

Another important facet of an online PR strategy, we note, is the need for integration with offline strategies. Implementing a public relations program or communication without integrating the online forum is a disservice to the brand. It's critical for the brand that is portrayed in traditional advertising in print and broadcast to be in line with what's being communicated online. Offline PR programs that increase awareness need to appear in the online forum as well. Even though brands find that they might reach different demographics online, the overall brand message needs to be consistent. Audiences who encounter offline PR receive a reinforced message when the Web site focuses on similar information. This crossover is being facilitated by the spread of high-speed Internet access, which will bring a convergence with TV and the ability to strengthen brand identity by using the same video on TV and on the Internet.

Finally, no aspect of Internet business can be discussed without proper attention to customer privacy. No one, from the technical personnel tracking site statistics to the marketing professionals eager to create customized features to the PR people responding to e-mailed queries, should overlook the tremendous importance that many people place on their personal privacy. A law governing information gathering from children is already on the books in the United States and more laws could be on the way. The European Community, meanwhile, has promulgated tough privacy regulations that affect U.S. companies operating overseas. PR people need to acknowledge the privacy of people's e-mail addresses, for example, by not sending mass mailings in which all the recipients' addresses are visible. Even more important, however, PR catastrophes can be averted if PR people assure that privacy policies are posted online and are being followed by employees and contractors. Customer data can be used for innovations like personalization that promise to improve online experiences, but companies must be sure to have consumers' permission before rolling out such innovations.

As we bring *The New PR Toolkit* to a close, we reflect on the tremendous change the Internet has made in the abilities of PR professionals to serve their constituents at any time, day or night. Although some might pine for the day when they had more control over how their clients were being discussed and perceived, there's no going back. A new communications channel has been born and we are all left to change with the times and ensure that we're doing all that we can to see that our clients are portrayed in as positive a way as merited. Some resistance to change is natural, but the new toolkit must be embraced as a means to move forward aggressively, thereby redefining the P in PR to mean "proactive."

With the end of the Internet frenzy and the onset of tough economic times, no one, not even deep-pocketed brands like Procter & Gamble or General Electric, is going to throw unlimited dollars at their online efforts. PR professionals need to ensure that what's spent is spent correctly by being proactive, doing accurate research, developing the appropriate strategies, staying on top of their execution, and managing a brand's reputation to guarantee the best possible outcomes for their clients.

I LAYING THE GROUNDWORK

1 THE 21ST-CENTURY AUDIENCE

➤ The business world is faster and less forgiving.

➤ The Internet makes PR materials available 24/7.

➤ Users' comfort levels with technology still vary.

N o one active in public relations since 1995 needs to be reminded how dramatically the profession has been changed. A key question is whether the change has been for the better or for the worse.

It can certainly be argued that the emphasis on speed that has accompanied the spread of the Internet has left us all feeling a little cheated in some ways. Brevity is king. Two-page press releases have been replaced by two-paragraph e-mails aimed at capturing the fleeting attention of overworked journalists, many of whom now serve print and online masters, churning out updates for their Web sites in addition to regular duties for a newspaper, magazine, or broadcast organization. Fewer journalists have time for business lunches, and even phone conversations aimed at uncovering story interests and building relationships seem harder to fit in. The standard question, "Is now a good time to talk?" almost isn't worth asking. "E-mail me" is the new mantra, but breaking through a journalist's e-mail clutter is a challenge unto itself.

The Internet has also fostered a self-serve attitude among journalists, analysts, and other constituents. All of them want immediate access on the Web to the latest information about every aspect of a client—from customer list to the CEO's biography.

This use of the Web helps PR people because our releases and other documents are available 24/7 to journalists around the world who might be interested in our clients, but it afflicts many of us with an unsettling loss of control. In the past, details about upcoming coverage could often be gleaned from journalists who called to request press kits. This interaction often gave us a better chance to influence that coverage in ways beneficial to our clients. Nowadays, we hope that those reading our releases and other materials online will call if they have questions, but we can't be sure that they will, and we end up feeling a little less certain that we know what's coming.

The Internet also has PR people working harder because we're exposed to the public in ways that didn't exist before. Because we're often the only ones whose telephone numbers are listed on a client's Web site, we hear from Internet users about lots of things beyond our control: bad links, unavailable files, or pages that load improperly. Suddenly, public relations is being mistaken for customer service. We're likely to hear from anyone who's had a bad experience with a client—from unhappy customers to disgruntled employees. All of this requires our time in making sure such messages get to the appropriate recipients. We've heard from executives, for example, who have asked their PR agencies to remove their names from the news releases on their company's Web site. One executive, in particular said that listing his contact information on the releases that went out over the wire was fine, but he didn't want any more cell phone calls over the weekend from Web surfers.

We're sure you have many more Internet-inspired headaches that can be added to this list, but none of them can persuade us that the Internet has changed the PR business for the worse. It's been quite an adjustment and an educational process for the PR pros and clients alike. However, we steadfastly believe that PR professionals are working more efficiently and effectively because of the Internet. It has brought the profession a collection of powerful tools for public relations that promises to become only broader and more useful in the future.

POWERFUL TOOLS

As noted earlier, the simple extension of the business day that the Internet has made possible is an advancement, the impact of which seems impossible to overestimate. Your clients' stories exist on their Web sites, ready for retrieval by anyone who types their name into a search engine. A reporter on a tight deadline who has heard of a client can get a pretty good picture of that company—and possibly include them in his or her copy—regardless of whether he or she is writing in London or Tokyo while the United States sleeps. Similarly, the asynchronous nature of e-mail means that we can communicate about our clients and their brands with people across the street or around the world without wasting hours playing endless games of telephone tag or worrying about timely delivery of press kits.

The Internet is also the most powerful research tool ever invented, offering us the opportunity to quickly assess our clients' positioning in their markets and their competitors. A simple search on Yahoo! Finance can tell us what a competitor has announced and how it's playing in the press. Services like MediaMap, PressAccess, and Bacon's help us keep up with the constantly changing personnel and beat assignments in most newsrooms so that list generation is an easy, accurate, and painless process. Other services like EdCal can tell us of planned stories that might be appropriate for our clients. Innovations like ProfNet have sprung up that enable us to get the top executives of clients listed in databases of experts that reporters often use in their search for sources.

Although many PR professionals still struggle to stock their clients' online pressrooms or to find the right subject line for an e-mailed release, many have used the tools with great success. One example is the PR and advertising campaign for About (*about.com*) when it changed its name from Mining Company in 1999. A series of mysterious, good-humored e-mail releases helped build suspense among reporters and analysts and attracted attention to the name change. Another effective e-mail campaign was pulled off by Peter Shenkman of the Geek Factory on behalf of SportsBrain, a maker of a device that joggers can use to keep track of how far they've run. Shankman's "Do you want to run with me?" subject line had him running more miles than he ever expected with media outlets including *The New York Times, The Today Show*, and *Entrepreneur* to name a few. PR21, the agency representing Apartments.com (*apartments.com*), an apartment-finding site, also taught us a few lessons about effective online PR with its campaign to identify the messiest college apartment. Video releases and the Apartments.com Web site kept attention on the contest, which offered a $10,000 prize, and won coverage in 440 print stories, 245 TV stories, and on 47 radio stations.

Dot-Com Lessons

The online companies About and Apartments.com were both still in business at this writing, but many other dot-coms that helped pioneer Internet tools for PR have passed from the scene. It's enough of a trend to cause more than a few people to wonder if there is any correlation between aggressive online PR and business failure. How much blame should PR people be assessed for the dot-com collapse?

Our answer is little or none. Although some PR folks might have stretched the truth at times in describing the capabilities of a few dot-com startups, the sector rose and fell because of the newness of the Internet and the wild expectations of analysts and investors. Dot-com faith translated into big initial public offerings (IPOs), which drove more investors and entrepreneurs into the market with business plans often less well baked than the ones that had come before them. Writing business plans on napkins should have been a first warning.

One PR veteran who shares this view is Melody Haller, president of Antenna Group, a San Francisco agency that represented many dot-com customers and continues to work with technology companies such as WebEx and NanoMuscle. She compares the dot-com frenzy to earlier stock market giddiness in both the software and hardware industries. "I think everybody was overselling everything," she recalls. "I had the experience of journalists writing things about our clients that were more breathless than what we promoted to them."

Haller says the craziness of the dot-com frenzy is easy to understand when she considers her own early involvement in Yahoo! Playing conservatively and selling her pre-IPO shares to Softbank for $12.50 a share cost her about $50 million, she estimates, citing Yahoo!'s incredible run-up. Such experiences, she notes, trained her and others like her to be more optimistic about the startups that followed. The market, says Haller, "punished you for having realistic expectations and it punished you very, very painfully."

An important difference between Yahoo! and the many dot-coms that have since failed, Haller contends, is that it was a solid business when it went public, having attracted 1 million users before the company was even founded. To the extent that public relations played a role in its success, Haller credits an old, tried-and-true strategy of featuring the personal stories of top executives and positioning them as "poster children" for the fast-growing universe of Internet users. In Yahoo!'s case, Jerry Yang and David Filo happened to be graduate students who had started the Web portal on Stanford University's computers. Haller says she might have sent some e-mails to reporters she thought would be interested in Yang and Filo, but e-mail was just a tool and not central to the overall strategy of making the two young founders accessible to the press. Even as e-mail has become more integral to the business of Antenna Group, Haller says she still takes pains to personalize pitches rather than broadcast them to long lists of reporters. She is also widely recognized for hosting "dinner salons" that bring journalists and her clients together in the flesh.

KNOW YOUR AUDIENCE

Such examples from Haller and other practitioners only reinforce our conviction that the key to successful online public relations is to integrate new tools into old-school, back-to-basics strategies. Our goal as PR professionals is to represent clients in the best light regardless of whether it's in print, on television, or on a computer screen. Being proactive starts with knowing your audience and how perceptions change over time. The steps to take to reach these segments still need the same careful consideration used in years past. Public relations is built on relationships. Internet or not, speed of light or Pony Express, you cannot disregard the fact that relationships take nurturing and understanding of needs. As such, communication must be tailored and incredibly specific despite the temptation many feel to go online with mass, untargeted information.

The strategies, therefore, need to be laid down on top of an important groundwork, which includes determining the makeup and interests of a client's audience. Are the reporters and analysts who visit online pressrooms any different from their colleagues who still prefer faxes? What about the members of the general public surfing through a client's Web site? What are they looking for? Are they generally older, younger, or otherwise demographically different from the company's typical customer?

We strongly recommend a close relationship between a company's PR operations and its Web site. If public relations professionals are not in charge of the site, they should be, at the least, members of whatever committees are convened to discuss site design and functionality. Communication professionals and information technology (IT) departments must align. You should argue loudly for easy access to information in place of flashy graphics that often delay Web users from getting the data they want. You should also keep a careful eye on a site's maintenance to make sure that the site represents the company in the best light. Finally, public relations people must be in a position to learn from what people are doing on a client's Web site to improve their interactions with the site. This means that Web log data showing how people entered a site, what they searched for, the documents they looked at, and the time spent looking at each one, must be shared with PR folks if the sites are to be made more useful to reporters, analysts, prospective customers, or any other cybervisitors.

One important factor to remember in understanding your client's online audience is that people are at very different stages of technology acceptance. Scholars who study the adoption of innovations have created the following labels to describe the spectrum of technology users:[1]

- **Innovators.** Often young and mobile, the members of this group embrace technology early on and were right there at the birth of the commercial Internet, jumping on the bandwagon with creative ideas. The innovators might also be classified as the group that immediately bought stock in Yahoo!, seeing the search engine as a valuable and groundbreaking tool in the Internet's future. Innovators want to see Web sites push the envelope in terms of utilizing new technology.

- **Early adopters.** Also young and mobile, but a little less prone to taking risks than are innovators, the early adopters were also on the Internet early, helping to fuel the growth of Amazon.com and eBay and willing to test the waters of online banking. This group is also quick to use e-mail and frowns at the hassle of snail mail. Early adopters are not afraid to complete online registration forms to receive free gifts and promotional offers from their favorite brands.

- **Early majority.** This group enjoys the speed and usefulness of the Internet for research and news and for corresponding with friends and family (often instant messaging with friends and family from the office). The early majority are much more cautious than the early adopters, as they require quite a bit more information and prompting to use the Internet in all of its capacities.

---

1. Cateora, Philip R., and Graham, John L. *International Marketing* (10th ed.). New York: McGraw Hill, 1996.

■ **Late majority.** Altogether different from any of the previous groups, the members of the late majority are generally overly suspicious of new ideas and did not embrace Internet technology until they were convinced of the solid benefits the medium offers, such as savings on long-distance phone charges. The late majority is usually comprised of older audiences (middle-aged to senior citizens) who look to preceding groups (and younger generations) for approval and safety when it comes to use of the medium.

■ **Laggards.** A group that clearly does not want to be bothered with the Internet, laggards are typically senior citizens who are content to rely on their traditional means for retrieving information. The telephone book will always be a guiding reference for this group. Although some might lack the economic means to purchase a computer or Internet access, many are also concerned about privacy and they are not eager to have their personal preferences tracked through cyberspace.

While there are exceptions on both sides of the Internet spectrum, it is pretty safe to say that many journalists and analysts fall into the early majority category and are willing to test drive new online features, like applets for graphing financial data, that promise to help them do their jobs better. Some innovations like Webcasts, however, can be problematic because of firewall and bandwidth issues related to the corporate networks of media companies, which are often not on the cutting edge.

Journalists and analysts have also been through the dot-com collapse and taken their share of criticism for helping to feed the investing frenzy before the crash. Regardless of whether such criticism is deserved, it's fair to say that both groups have emerged more skeptical. Reporters are tired of hearing about tiny startups promising to revolutionize some aspect of American business. Their editors, stung by the criticism of dot-com coverage and seeking to fill fewer magazine or newspaper pages in a slow economy, are asking much tougher questions about story ideas than they ever did in the late 1990s.

PR professionals must be capable of providing solid information up front about a company's business plan, financing, and executive leadership just to get a journalist interested in possibly pursuing a story. Providing such information online is only going to help your chances of getting that attention. Archives of press releases that chronicle the company's development and its customer wins can also be assets in swaying a journalist who is doing due diligence of potential story subjects and could very well be doing it long after regular business hours.

When it comes to members of the general public who are visiting a client's Web site, knowing the makeup of your online audience is important because fancy online features intended to impress innovators might turn off the less technologically astute. At the same time, a company positioning itself as a technology leader needs to display some of its prowess and not develop the simplest of sites. Knowing your audience can also tell you how willing your online visitors might be to trade some of their privacy for surfing experiences that are more customized to their interests. Lexis-Nexis, which provides searchable databases for lawyers, government officials, and corporate executives, learned this lesson the hard way during its early days online. The company ignored privacy complaints of one of its users who did not like a new service that disclosed the Social Security numbers of prominent people. After countless efforts to be heard, this woman decided to take her complaints to the Internet and posted negative comments on a message board. The message spread like wildfire as it was picked up by at least 300 other Web sites. With the decision to not squash the negative communication or aggressively respond to it, Lexis-Nexis still received calls from reporters a year after the woman first spoke out.

On the other hand, a good example of how a company displayed sensitivity to the worries of its customers can be found in Ask Jeeves' handling of customers of E-tours, a company it acquired in May 2001. The E-tours site had provided members with points for agreeing to take tours of Web sites that were supposed to fit with their interests. The purchase by Jeeves and a name change to Jeeves' Tours marked the end of the points program and members were offered the opportunity to become involved with Qool.com, an Internet auction site that is known as "the Internet's first and only 'free auction' site."[2] Because the new alliance allowed visitors to transfer points from the old program, Jeeves' Tours wanted to provide its audience with Qool.com's privacy policy. An e-mail update went out to all of the Jeeves' Tours members with a link to view Qool.com's privacy policy on the Web. Unfortunately, there were some technical difficulties and the information was difficult to access. However, when inquiries were made to Jeeves' Tours, the brand expeditiously e-mailed the privacy policy to its users. The policy was thorough and complete, with information about children's data, what type of information is collected, why it is collected, registration and membership services, and security and safeguard measures. This brand was proactive in its efforts, realizing the core membership group (the members of the late majority) was skeptical about Internet privacy issues. Forwarding privacy policies before the customer asked for them qualifies Jeeves' Tours for our gold star for smart public relations and brand management on the Internet.

Unfortunately, too many dot-coms failed to understand their audiences or care about their technology comfort levels. What's the use of offering technology if the visitor does not know how to access it, maneuver through it, or distrusts it? Web experiences too often did not match up with the hype surrounding dot-coms and brands were tarnished by that fact that customers were left feeling that promises had been broken. This, indeed, is counterproductive to the PR professional who aims to build the image and protect the brand's reputation.

PR professionals might not have been the leaders of the dot-com doom, but not taking the time to realize and apply the tried and true strategies that worked so well in the past certainly did not benefit their brands. There are simply no substitutes for research and careful planning as we seek to address the needs of 21st-Century audiences.

In the next chapter, our focus is on what researchers tell us about Internet users as we try to help you lay that groundwork for your clients' or your own company's Internet initiatives.

---

2.   E-Tour and Ask Jeeves member update, August 13, 2001.

2 IDENTIFYING AUDIENCE TRENDS

➤ The online population is large and growing.
➤ An increasingly diverse population is doing serious research online.
➤ The public wants no barriers between companies' online and offline appearance.

A smart first step in laying the groundwork for making better use of the Internet for public relations is to understand what researchers have already learned about the online population. Does it really make sense to tie a promotional campaign for a maker of denture adhesive to a Web site contest or sweepstakes? Well, maybe not today, but three years from now it might. What about your plan for loading up your client's Web site with all of its TV commercials and video of its recent press conferences? Will the video attract enough users to justify the cost of putting it online? The anticipated spread of high-speed Internet access seems to indicate that now's the time to get those videos racked up and ready to roll.

There is certainly no shortage of data to plow through in your search for answers to these questions and others—and no scarcity of research organizations like Jupiter Media Metrix, Nielsen//NetRatings, Gartner, or IDC looking to sell you data customized to fit your interests. This secondary data can answer some of your research questions and help you plan better and more cost effectively for your own primary data gathering.

Our goal with this chapter is to help you fill in the blanks as best you can before going out to hire a research firm, or prior to employing your own resources in the research process. Knowing the latest audience trends should help you in determining what online tools to use in reaching out to your clients' target audiences and how to better tailor a branded message based on online usage and surfing habits.

A LARGE AUDIENCE...

All figures bandied about concerning the numbers of people on the Internet must be regarded with some skepticism because an accurate count is clearly impossible. There is no central authority in charge of the Internet and an organization that links its computers to the Internet does not have to declare to anyone whether it has granted Internet access to 30 employees or 30,000. The same is true of companies that provide access to individuals in their homes. America Online is believed to be the giant in the field with more than 35 million subscribers in late 2002, but it is impossible to know how many people have accounts with untold numbers of smaller service providers in obscure corners of the globe—or even in the United States.

Nevertheless, researchers do the best they can. The number of people logging on through U.S. households in September 2001 was 168.4 million, according to Nielsen//NetRatings. The same company estimated that 42.7 million people logged on through their workplaces in that same month, but some number of them were undoubtedly also counted in the tally of at-home users.

A closer look at the weekly activity data that Nielsen//NetRatings compiled from its panels of allegedly representative U.S. Internet users tells us people did nearly twice as much surfing at work (six hours, 17 minutes) during the week that started August 26, 2001 than they did at home (three hours,

12 minutes). Although the different groups each spent about a half-hour during each surfing session, the greater number of sessions for workers enabled them to cover 14 different sites in a week as opposed to six for at-home surfers (see Tables 2-1 and 2-2).

TABLE 2-1   Average Web Use at Work, August 26–September 2, 2001

No. of sessions per week	12
No. of unique sites visited	14
Time spent per week	6:17:02
Time spent per session	32:05
Duration of a page viewed	00:58
Active Internet universe	35,269,988
Internet universe estimate	42,719,009

Source: Nielsen//NetRatings

TABLE 2-2   Average Web Use at Home, August 26–September 2, 2001

No. of sessions per week	6
No. of unique sites visited	6
Time spent per week	3:12:03
Time spent per session	31:32
Duration of a page viewed	00:51
Active Internet universe	72,425,112
Internet universe estimate	168,392,667

Source: Nielsen//NetRatings

...AND GROWING

The collapse of so many dot-coms has caused some observers of the Internet to question whether it would continue its meteoric growth in usership. The Pew Internet & American Life Project tackled that question during the darkest days of the Internet market downturn, comparing the makeup of Internet users at the end of 2000 to what it had been in the spring of that year. Pew's results (see Table 2-3) indicated big growth in numbers of Internet users in all demographic groups. For example, three-quarters of Americans between 18 and 29 years old were online, as were nearly two-thirds of those between 30 and 49. Huge majorities of people earning more than $30,000 a year were also online, but there was also significant growth in Internet use among those below that income level.

TABLE 2-3   Growth of Internet Population (Percentage of Each Group Online)

ONLINE GROUP	SPRING 2000 (%)	LATE 2000 (%)
All Adults	47	56
Men	50	58
Women	45	54
Whites	49	57
Blacks	35	43
Hispanics	40	47
Parents of children under 18	55	66
Nonparents	43	50
Age Cohorts		
18–29	61	75
30–49	57	65
50–64	41	51
65+	12	15
Income Brackets		
Under $30K	28	38
$30K–$50K	50	64
$50K–$75K	67	72
$75K+	79	82
Education Levels		
High school or less	28	39
Some college	62	71
College degree or more	76	82

Source: Pew Internet & American Life Project Surveys, May–June and November–December 2000. Margin of error is ±3%.

The Pew project took another shot at assessing the impact of the dot-com collapse on Internet use in early 2001, asking survey participants whether their Internet use had risen or declined in the previous six months. The results were encouraging for Internet communicators, showing that 29 percent of Internet users were online more than before, 54 percent were holding steady, and only 17 percent said they were online less often.

Among those online more than they had been in the past, their most common explanation was that the Internet had become essential for their work or schooling. The second largest group said they had simply found more things to do on the Internet. Indeed, the survey found that 51 percent of those connected to the Internet at work said they were online several times a day, up from 40 percent in a Pew survey taken one year earlier.

Alternatively, the small group who said they spent less time online blamed that on being less interested in what they had been doing online and on the time pressures of daily life. A few said they found the Internet to be neither useful nor worthwhile, which suggests to us that they might have been turned off by Web sites that promised a lot more than they delivered, a too-common phenomenon during the heyday of the dot-com era. Finally, a small number of those who spent less time online told Pew that they were still fans of the Internet, but had become more efficient in their use of it and had faster connections that liberated them from long sessions waiting for pages to download.

WHAT THEY'RE DOING

Any of us familiar with the Internet probably don't have too much difficulty figuring out what people are doing with their time spent online. The Pew study that compared activities in late 2000 to those in the spring of that year found that large and growing majorities of Internet users said they had used the Internet to seek hobby information, to browse for

fun, and to get news. Perhaps most important to public relations professionals were the findings that more than half of
those surveyed were using the Internet for purchases and for
job-related research, clear indications that business decisions
are being influenced by visits to corporate Web sites (see Table
2-4). Such findings support our strongly held belief that public
relations professionals need to be incorporating current PR
programs into a client's Web site or your own in-house PR,
posting the latest news online, and taking full control of the
site's online newsroom.

TABLE 2-4   Internet Activities (Percentage of Users Who Have Reported Doing the Following Online)

ACTIVITY	SPRING 2000 (%)	LATE 2000 (%)
Look for hobby information	71	79
Browse for fun	61	68
Buy a product	46	52
Get news	60	63
Get medical information	55	57
Do research for their jobs	50	52
Get financial information	43	45
Buy or sell stocks	12	14

Source: *Pew Internet & American Life Project Surveys, May–June and November–December 2000. Margin of error is ±3%.*

ONLINE VETS DO MORE

Pew's research also reveals something interesting related
to people in the different stages of technology adoption that we
identified in Chapter 1. Those who have been online at least
three years—a constituency that includes old-time computer
fans and Gen-Xers who grew up with the Internet—are probably most likely to be labeled innovators and early adopters and
are the most loyal to the Internet and likely to consider it
essential to their lives. Nearly 60 percent of online veterans

surveyed in early 2001 said they would miss the Internet "a lot" if it they lost access, whereas that sentiment was shared by only 29 percent of those who had gone online in the previous six months. This allegiance to the Internet is understandable (see Table 2-5) considering that Pew's research found that online vets were the most likely to be availing themselves of the Internet's many services in greater numbers than newcomers, who were more likely to go online primarily to exchange e-mail or to browse for fun. Such findings reinforce our point in Chapter 1 that public relations professionals need to know the technology comfort level of the people interacting with their clients online. They must also be ready to offer more features when it is determined that the audience has significant numbers of technologically savvy users who are actively using the Internet to make their lives easier and more productive.

TABLE 2-5 Veterans Compared to Newcomers

ACTIVITY	VETERANS (%)	NEWCOMERS (%)
Go online just for fun	64	61
Visit an adult site	15	14
Send or read e-mail	97	88
Search for the answer to a specific question	87	60
Look for info on hobbies	83	64
Get news online	78	44
Look for job-related information	65	30
Buy a product	64	31
Look for health-related information	63	47
Look for financial information	54	21
Listen to music online	45	33
Download music	33	27
Buy or sell stocks	18	3

Source: Pew Internet & American Life Project Tracking Survey, February 2001. Margin of error is ±3 percent.

Meanwhile, a separate research study by the Pew Internet & American Life Project has found that young people between the ages of 12 and 17 engage in a wide variety of online activities, ranging from heavy use of entertainment sites to product research (see Table 2-6). Such trends should be of interest to anyone serving a client who is targeting young consumers, but there is also a lesson here for public relations professionals who want to anticipate some things about the young journalists they'll be dealing with in just a few years. For one thing, they are big users of instant messaging programs, such as AOL

TABLE 2-6   What Teens Are Doing (Percentage Who Have Used the Net for the Following Activities)

ACTIVITY	PERCENT
Send or read e-mail	92
Surf the Web for fun	84
Visit an entertainment site	83
Send an instant message	74
Look for information on hobbies	69
Get news	68
Play or download a game	66
Research a product or service before buying it	66
Listen to music online	59
Visit a chat room	55
Download music files	53
Check sports scores	47
Visit a site for a club or team that they are a member of	39
Got to site where they can express opinions	38
Buy something	31
Visit sites for trading or selling things	31
Look for health-related information	26
Create a Web page	24
Look for info on a topic that is hard to talk about	18

Source: Pew Internet & American Life Project Teens and Parents Survey, November–December 2000. Margin of error is ±4 percent.

Instant Messenger, which allow Internet users to communicate in real time with correspondents who are on the Internet at the same time. Should PR people be preparing to use instant messaging as a vehicle for distributing story pitches? Given the technology's ability to interrupt and intrude on what a journalist is doing, we're inclined to recommend limiting its use to those cases in which you have the permission of the journalist. It's not hard to imagine that some reporters who follow one of your clients' brands or your own company's brand very closely might be willing to divulge their instant messenger names to you if they know the technology will be used only for making them aware of unscheduled important announcements, like the resignation of a CEO. Other reporters, though, are likely to consider their instant messenger names to be off-limits to anyone outside their tight circle of friends and family members. Technology is definitely changing the rules of the game that we play and we will all have to sort out what acceptable practices are in this new environment. That's a topic we'll tackle in a future chapter.

BROADBAND IS COMING

Absent from most research about what people are doing online is any mention of bandwidth-hungry applications, like downloading video. Its oversight is primarily the result of the Internet's current limited capacity, which is rapidly improving. It is a development that should cause more public relations professionals to consider putting Webcasts of press conferences online along with promotional videos or TV commercials that could help tie together images of a client in the online and offline worlds. In theory, a Webcast is a PR person's ideal tool because it offers the ability to have large groups view a program to build brand awareness. Technical glitches, inadequate bandwidth, and firewall problems in many media companies have given Webcasts a bad name, but that situation is changing fairly quickly. There is also renewed interest in the technology due to cost and security concerns related to business travel. A Nielsen//NetRatings report issued in October

2001 found that 21 million people had used the Internet in their workplace to view streaming media within the previous month, an increase of 21 percent from the same month in 2000. Those looking at streaming video represented 56 percent of all Internet users at work, which Jarvis Mak, a NetRatings senior Internet analyst, described as "a critical mass."[1]

Access to broadband connections has also been growing in U.S. households as Digital Subscriber Line (DSL) and cable modem service has become more widely available. Jupiter Media Metrix said in a report in late 2000 that the growth seen so far was slow compared to what will happen as telephone and cable carriers bid prices down from the $49-a-month level to amounts more in line with what people are willing to spend for traditional dial-up Internet access. Jupiter said the 8.6 million households with broadband access would grow to 28.8 million in 2005 (see Table 2-7).

TABLE 2-7   Broadband Household Projections (In Millions)

	1999	2000	2001	2002	2003	2004
No. of Households	1.8	4.8	8.6	13.3	18.5	23.8

Source: Jupiter Research, a division of Jupitermedia Corporation. Originally published November 2000.

ONLINE-OFFLINE TRANSPARENCY

One final audience trend worth calling to the attention of public relations professionals is the conclusion reached in several research reports about the desire of Internet users to interact with a company's online and offline operations as transparently as possible. This means that Internet users want the perception of the company that they get online to be consistent with what they experience in the stores. They want to

1.   Nielsen//NetRatings press release, October 11, 2001.

be able to buy something from the Web site and return it in a local store without having to wait in line at the post office to mail it back to the Web site's distribution center.

A March 2001 Jupiter Media Metrix study, for example, found that 83 percent of online buyers said they would like to be able to return online purchases at offline stores. Additionally, 59 percent of respondents said that they would like to order a product online and pick it up at an offline store. However, Jupiter analysts found that only 18 percent of multichannel retailers offered in-store pickup of items ordered online. Jupiter also found that 67 percent of online buyers said they expected store staff members to be able to view their online account information, which is rarely possible. "Multichannel retailers have been treating their online and offline businesses as separate entities, but that's not what consumers want," concluded Jupiter analyst David Daniels.[2]

Another Jupiter study released in July 2001 hammered on the same point, noting that young consumers in particular were fond of doing research online and then purchasing products in stores. Teens generally don't have credit cards, which are needed for online purchases, but their buying decisions are undoubtedly influenced by what they are learning through searches of Amazon.com and other sites, Jupiter said. "Since so few teenagers purchase online, the Web should be used as an additional means of branding and information dissemination," said Jupiter analyst Jared Blank. "Players who do this well ensure that their customer communications, whether it's informational or promotional, share the same messaging on the Web, in their catalogs, and in their stores."[3]

The lesson for public relations professionals, therefore, is to push hard to break down barriers within the companies you are working with to ensure that their public faces and pronouncements are consistent, regardless of whether they're communicating online or offline.

---

2. Jupiter Media Metrix press release, March 21, 2001.
3. Jupiter Media Metrix press release, July 18, 2001.

We'd be remiss, however, if we failed to include at least some note of caution at this point given the public's demonstrated uneasiness with being watched too closely. Although consumers say they want to interact with online and offline arms of a company and generally embrace the notion of receiving specially targeted promotional offers, they also express huge concerns about the databases of personal information and purchasing histories that enable large retailers to offer such features. We'll talk more in Chapter 13 about the importance of having a prominent privacy statement that helps to explain your information practices.

In our next chapter, we aim to help you zero in on what, in particular, Internet users want from your Web site and those of your clients.

3 KNOWING WHAT YOUR PUBLIC WANTS

➤ Understanding customers' needs is still important.
➤ Thorough research is needed to meet customers' expectations.
➤ Continued research helps you refine your online approach.

◻ nce you've digested all that secondary research from NetRatings, Gartner, and their competitors, you'll probably be feeling ready to take the Internet by storm. We're sure you'll have ideas about how to communicate with reporters and consumers online given your knowledge about overall demographics of the online population, projections of high-speed access, and other factors. So, you're ready to get cracking, right?

Not so fast.

We think you've only just begun to lay the groundwork for effectively using the Internet for representing your client. What do you really know about what these Internet users want from your client? Understanding the needs of the audience you're communicating with is still a fundamental tenet of sound public relations regardless of whether you're reaching people online or offline. Unfortunately, it was one principle that was frequently overlooked during the height of dot-com mania. We can recall at least one uncomfortable situation at a PR industry meeting where we cited the need for continuing research into the needs of a client's constituents, only to have our suggestion met with blank stares and impatient sighs from other PR professionals in the room. Many of them were operating on Internet time, after all, and couldn't be bothered with too much research. "Deploy, deploy, deploy!" was their mantra. However, as we've noted previously, the end to Internet time is a good thing. We all need to take the time to understand more clearly what people are expecting from our clients online. Failing to meet their expectations amounts to a recipe for tarnishing a client's reputation—which is the ultimate sign of a PR person's failure.

UNDERSTANDING WHAT PEOPLE EXPECT OF YOUR CLIENT ONLINE

The different constituents of PR professionals should be considered separately in evaluating their needs. We should all have experience in trying to keep up with what reporters and analysts need. Knowing what a publication covers and how it approaches stories has always been important to PR people. However, the rise of the Internet should cause us to re-evaluate what we think we know about the interests of all those names in our media databases. Is this particular magazine still interested in the same type of stories now that it has a Web site that is updated daily with breaking news? Is there a separate staff responsible for the Web site? If there is only one editorial staff for Web and print products, is it possible that reporters might be more open to pitches for short, focused stories that could be developed quickly for the Web site? Is this reporter now also more willing to book press tour visits in his or her office given his or her increased deadline pressures and the tightness of travel budgets in lean times?

It's also worthwhile to keep up with how your media sources are feeling about Internet technology. Are the old-fashioned fax lovers now more willing to accept pitches via e-mail? What types of things do journalists and analysts expect to find on your client's Web site? Do they want a searchable database of old press releases? If so, how many years are sufficient? Are the journalists on your press list now willing and able to log on for Webcasts? Would they be interested in receiving a periodic e-mail newsletter that would update them on your client's notable achievements?

Keeping up with journalists' preferences is probably old hat for a lot of PR professionals and we'll talk more in Chapter 4 about new Internet tools that can help you get the job done. However, the new task brought on by the rise of the Internet is identifying the needs of potential customers and business partners who are interacting with your client's Web site or your company's Web site in the case of an in-house PR professional. As we noted in previous chapters, public relations is now more public than ever and it is important to protecting your client's reputation that you become aware of exactly what individuals are seeking from the client online so that you can satisfy those expectations.

FACTORS AFFECTING YOUR ONLINE COMMUNICATIONS STRATEGY

The late American psychologist Abraham Maslow was a pioneer in researching how people are driven by needs. He arranged needs in a hierarchy with lower level needs (physiological needs)—such as food, water, and shelter—needing to be satisfied before the higher level needs (self-actualization needs) such as self-development are reached. According to Maslow, when a person has satisfied a particular need, he or she strives to reach higher levels. Following Maslow's theory, it can be argued that every audience has a needs hierarchy that must be satisfied on some level if a company is going to make a positive impression on that audience. To satisfy needs on a higher level, communication and positive interaction with the brand must remain constant. This is not easy to achieve on the Internet, as many brands have experienced thus far. Technology can be unpredictable and often frustrating. Until the medium is perfected to suit every type of user from the innovator to even a laggard (if that's possible), the challenge to satisfy continually intensifies. With each passing day, groups are using the Internet more and expecting more from any brand with which they choose to interact.

Determining the needs of those interacting with your client online requires you to know something about the macro and micro environmental factors that shape their needs. The macro factors are the kinds of things that you can learn about through a review of the secondary research that we discussed in Chapter 2. They include indicators such as the following:

- **Demographic factors:** World population growth, population age mix, ethnic markets, educational groups, household patterns, and so on.

- **Economic factors:** Income distribution, debt, credit availability, and so on.

- **Technological factors:** Pace of technology, opportunity for innovation, increased regulation for technological change.

- **Political and legal environment:** Legislation affecting businesses, protection from unfair competition, consumer protection and privacy issues, and so on.

- **Social factors:** Audience views of themselves, views of others, views of society, and so on.

The micro environmental factors that shape your audience's needs are closely related to a person's general lifestyle and are gathered by using primary, firsthand research tools like online surveys of site visitors. These factors include the following:

- **Cultural factors:** Culture, subcultures, social class, and so on.

- **Social factors:** Reference groups, family, roles, status, and so on.

- **Personal factors:** Stage of the life cycle, occupation, economic circumstances, lifestyle, personality, and so on.

- **Psychological factors:** Motivation, perceptions, learning, beliefs, attitudes.

The relative importance of these various factors to your online communications strategy is going to vary based on the type of audience you're addressing. If you're developing a plan for a business-to-business company seeking to sell its widgets to manufacturers, it's probably less important to know about the lifestyles and personalities of your online visitors and more important to know about economic factors such as credit availability. On the other hand, someone crafting an online communications strategy for a consumer-oriented company, like a cosmetics retailer, would be very interested in knowing about the cultural factors affecting its online users. Such a company might want to know about the age, race, ethnicity, economic circumstances, and perceptions of its online visitors. We'll talk more in Chapter 5 about tools that can be used to gather this information, but our purpose here is to point out the types of information that you need to know to be a better online communicator.

ONGOING RESEARCH IS CRITICAL

We recognize that our devotion to thorough research might not necessarily be shared by all your clients—especially those most eager to get to market now and figure out audience characteristics later. We nevertheless urge you to press hard for such research not only for the benefit of crafting the PR message, but also to ensure the overall success of whatever the client is selling. Thinking through the needs of the intended audience is an important exercise in solidly positioning a company.

One useful approach to figuring out what users expect from your client's Web site is to consider a theory known as the "five levels of product benefits," which suggests that customers who come to you to fulfill a basic need can be retained as you demonstrate the ability to meet their needs as those needs become more complex.[1] An example commonly cited in textbooks such

1. Kotler, Philip, *Marketing Management (The New Millennium Edition)*, Prentice Hall, Upper Saddle River, NJ, 2000.

as Kotler's *Marketing Management: Millennium Edition* is based on the needs that hotels usually fulfill for their guests. This example explains that guests of a hotel come to stay for the most fundamental, core benefit, which is a place to sleep. The second level or *basic product* provides the hotel customer with the necessities, including a bed and a bathroom. The third level or the *expected product* is a step up toward more customer value with the customer expecting clean facilities and a room that is neat and tidy. The next level of satisfaction is the *augmented product*, a level that is meant to exceed customer expectations. A hotel room that includes HBO and Showtime and perhaps mints on a pillow might qualify as an augmented product. The final level of perceived customer value is the *potential product* or the level that seeks to be everything and more to its customer. At this level of satisfaction, the hotel guests are delighted at the great lengths the hotel goes to satisfy a variety of needs. However, as stated, with different levels of interaction by various groups of people, it is necessary for brands online to prepare to satisfy expectations of several groups, or know what it takes to satisfy that one group at all times.[2] Research is crucial to identify this information.

Let's take the example of a dot-com that launched in 1999 called RegionalHelpWanted.com (*regionalhelpwanted.com*). This is a pure e-brand that makes its money (yes, believe it or not, the e-brand makes money) by partnering with local radio broadcast stations to design, build, and maintain Web sites throughout the country. The goals of the regional sites are to capitalize on the fact that most help wanted advertising is local (not national) and to get radio's fair share of the daily newspapers' $8 billion in annual help wanted revenues. RegionalHelp-Wanted.com helped itself in market positioning by researching local audiences, including radio station owners, local merchants, and job-seeking candidates. If we were to apply the five levels of product benefits to this Internet brand it would break down in the following way:

---

2. Kotler, Philip, *Marketing Management (The New Millennium Edition)*, Prentice Hall, Upper Saddle River, NJ, 2000.

- **Core product:** RegionalHelpWanted.com sites allow job seekers to find opportunities and advertisers to post job listings.
- **Basic product:** Job seekers can navigate the site quickly to search for job opportunities locally and to post résumés. Recruiters can place ads and maintain recruiter account information easily.
- **Expected product:** A local employment site (the name gives the expectation) with easy instructions, quick access to information, and no lengthy registration process.
- **Augmented product:** A high level of customer service with the ability to click on a live chat to ask questions or contact a sales representative immediately. It's a simple process, as basic as reading a newspaper.
- **Potential product:** RegionalHelpWanted.com sites strive to offer better services for their customers and look to include additional services including real estate and classified ad listings.

Working with a client to consider how its offerings fit with the five levels of product benefits can be difficult because it can force a client to make some major decisions: What does the client want its brand to be? Which product level is the company aiming to satisfy? Where does the target audience sit on the spectrum of technological savviness? Can the client, for example, realistically hope to deliver an augmented product to an audience of innovators and early adopters?

Many brands launched on the Internet realized early on that they would not be able to provide augmented or potential products. They correctly tried to keep things simple, aiming to provide a reliable basic or expected product. However, many companies failed to see that their early customers were early adopters or early majority technology users who demanded increasingly sophisticated features on Web sites. They wanted more than catalog listings from an online retailer. They wanted photos of the items. They wanted the ability to customize merchandise. They wanted the ability to track their deliveries through FedEx or UPS. They wanted to be rewarded for their loyalty with points that could be used at other sites or for air travel. Then, on the other hand, there were brands that offered sophisticated features, such as Flash and Shockwave applications and 3D animation, and found out quickly that their audience did not find the glitz and glamour so appealing. In essence, they were looking for simple functionality and a better way to communicate with their favored brands.

Ultimately, many brands suffered great losses—losses that perhaps could have been avoided if appropriate research was done on audience needs, expectations, and technological understanding. Remember that a brand present on the Internet needs to communicate the same consistent message, design, and image. The brand must transmit the same value sought by its customers regardless of the communication channel. Building value is an inherent part of branding that is automatically tied to a company's image and reputation. There's not a moment when a PR person is not concerned about getting the right messages to the right audience and eliciting a positive public reaction as a result of the communication.

A good example of a brand that ventured onto the Internet and discovered early on how to satisfy its customers' needs is Ceridian, a business solutions company that developed a payroll and human resources administration service online for small businesses. Ceridian had a unit called MiniData that provided payroll services to small business primarily through telephone or facsimile communications. The start of the 1990s saw the advent of proprietary software, which enabled Ceridian's clients to have software on their computer systems to process payroll transactions via a modem using telephone lines. The launch of Powerpay (*powerpay.com*) took Ceridian's service to still a higher level by making it possible for clients to process payroll transactions anytime, anywhere, regardless of whether a computer was loaded with the proprietary software. Ceridian's extensive and ongoing research had enabled it to predict and meet the needs of its Internet-using customers. If we were to apply the five levels of product benefits to this Internet brand, it would break down this way:

- **Core product:** Simple payroll service.
- **Basic product:** Payroll with tax filing service.

- **Expected Product:** Customers receive a high level of accuracy, affordable payroll service rates, and timely delivery of checks for their employees (exceeding the expectations of the offline payroll service and living up to a historical promise).

- **Augmented product:** Via the Internet, customers have the ability to easily link to strategic partners for various opportunities and optimal services.

- **Potential product:** Expanding to include real-time services that are not available offline including a human resources system that connects to payroll (401k plan) and same-day reporting for easier discussion between clients and their accounting firms.

Ceridian's ability to satisfy its clients' needs and exceed expectations has resulted in ongoing relationships with the brand's stakeholders. Years of continuing focus group research and usability studies have led to many successes for the brand and positive public opinion.

Now that the online payroll service has been launched, is it necessary for Ceridian to continue to put so much emphasis on researching new Internet efforts? Should the company be investing in research as a means to preserve reputation, image, and the satisfaction level of users even after a brand is already successful? The answer again is yes, absolutely. Remember, once a promise, always a promise from that brand.

That's one reason why Microsoft's free e-mail service Hotmail has done well when so many other free ad-supported e-mail providers have failed. Hotmail is a recognized brand because it grew quickly as a result of its uncomplicated nature. It enables users to register promptly and maintain a free e-mail account through MSN.com. Over the past couple of years, MSN has cared about its image and the needs of the Hotmail subscribers. Such concern is evident with the frequent change of the Hotmail Web design for simplified operation. Use of Hotmail is convenient and it provides an easy means for users to organize incoming mail. The site downloads quickly (also typical of MSN) and encompasses a site layout and navigation that is self-explanatory and absolutely mindless to operate. The expectation for every user is ease of use. Clearly, Microsoft has not skimped on whatever research has been needed to meet these expectations.

Another good example of a company that employs research and changes with the needs of its audience is 1-800-GIFT CERTIFICATE (*800giftcertificate.com*), a brand that prides itself on taking the time to know its customers. Like many dot-coms, 1-800-GIFT CERTIFICATE launched its site during the Internet boom, in hopes of attracting and retain a large consumer audience. "It didn't take long for us to revise the site," stated Dan Horne, director of research. "We quickly got into the habit of evaluating what others did. We're very fortunate to have people on board with talent and who work hard to analyze and tweak the site." 1-800-GIFT CERTIFICATE did not let the time pressures of being a startup affect its ability to build a functionally successful site. However, despite the functionality, Horne discussed with us how through continued research, 1-800-GIFT CERTIFICATE changed its audience focus from a consumer-oriented site to a corporate, business-minded site.

As the company grew, along with the growth came more resources. Horne felt early on that the company needed a consistent look and feel to all customer groups and that in the beginning it was trying to be everything all at once. In addition, although the company was positive about the product offering, what was exciting to management was not necessarily exciting to customers. 1-800-GIFT CERTIFICATE took the time to evaluate customer habits and click-through rates. "Every person in the company was on the telephone talking to customers—even company president Mike Dermer," stated Horne. The information from customer feedback and site traffic led to a new direction for the company.

1-800-GIFT CERTIFICATE relaunched its Web site in December 2001. Simplicity and a clean look and feel are the most apparent changes. Management decided that all the fancy features (e.g., holiday reminders and gift calendars) were not necessary. "They just slowed the customer down," Horne stated. It was at this point that 1-800-GIFT CERTIFI-

CATE began the shift of audience focus. The company found that corporate audiences made up almost 90 percent of the company's site traffic. However, there were still some consumer elements that remained. The revamped site is easy for the business purchaser to get in and get out of quickly and easily. Horne also noted that corporate demo programs including Points Express were especially attractive to business buyers.

1-800-GIFT CERTIFICATE is a great example of a company that was fortunate to realize early the importance of research and how to apply the findings to its Web site design. "We were very careful all the way through. Most companies that start out on the Internet work in a vacuum. Not us, we were constantly in contact with the customers," stated Horne. "And, all through the process, many people were involved," he added. Horne explained that this slower, more conservative approach led to a thought process that more dot-coms should have adhered to. It's fine to step back, wait a minute, and determine if there is value to the customer. Horne, who has a PhD in marketing research, described 1-800-GIFT CERTIFICATE as a logical company that is theoretically driven. "It's the way that academia [theory] and business should work together and it certainly worked for our company."

Before getting on with our discussion of the tools that can aid you in researching the needs of reporters (Chapter 4), we'll reiterate once more the need for PR professionals to think in broader terms in the new Internet age. Public relations has to be about more than just information dissemination because the Internet can accomplish that task so well on its own. PR is increasingly about reputation management. To serve their clients well, PR professionals must have access to the research that's needed to target the right messages to the right audiences and then to monitor those messages. At all times, research intelligence must continually be added to the communication process.

4 KNOWING WHAT THE NEWS MEDIA WANT

➤ Web sites of news organizations tell you what they cover.

➤ Online media guides supercede their paper ancestors.

➤ Newsletters and other resources can help you refine your approach.

Wouldn't it be wonderful if every journalist that you pitched took a moment to thank you for your valuable time, effort, and information? Imagine if every time you pitched an editor or producer, your client fit perfectly into his or her print story or broadcast program—impeccable timing! Better yet, could you envision getting a cover story for your client month after month because you did your homework?

Now wake up. Let's come back to reality.

From experience, we all know that great successes do not occur for every PR professional every day. However, we also know that success often comes from building solid relationships with journalists, and such relationships can be built more quickly by using the Internet to gather more detailed information about the publications or broadcasts you are targeting and about the journalists themselves. A PR person who demonstrates familiarity with the work of the people he or she is contacting is always going to be taken more seriously.

This topic calls to mind an embarrassing story that we're sure is similar to experiences that many public relations professionals have had at some point in their careers. A young woman was excited to get a correspondent's attention at *The Journal of Commerce*. The correspondent was interested in her client, a firm that specialized in investigating white-collar crime, embezzlement, and espionage. The young woman had used *Burrelle's Media Guides* at the time to research the newspaper, a century-old publication based in New York City. The directory information was helpful, but certainly not updated to reflect the changes in the media business. Only a week earlier she had received a lead from another editor of a logistics publication who recommended she call *The Journal of Commerce*. So, with a referral name (we all do a little name dropping here and there) and all of her prior research, she thought she had a sure ticket to an editorial placement. She felt she was ready to talk with the correspondent to pitch her client's business. When she had the correspondent on the telephone, the conversation started out smoothly. He was asking her questions about her client's involvement in undercover operations and she was fielding the questions as well as any knowledgeable professional would. However, the conversation took a turn for the worse when the young woman offered some outdated information that she had obtained from the media guide to the correspondent. He, in turn, stated in a sharpened tone, "You're lucky my editor did not hear you say that . . . don't you follow our publication? We've made so many changes." He went on to further degrade her and said, "My editor would have scrapped this article by now. That's what's wrong with you PR people. You don't do your research but expect us to use you for a story in our publication." The young woman, feeling terrible about the turn of events, apologized to the correspondent (for lack of anything better to do) and hung up the telephone, realizing that pitching a correspondent went beyond the simple information listed in a *Burrelle's* book. It was a rude awakening. Until that day, she thought she had done her homework.

The lesson learned in this scenario is that you can never have enough information about your audience and finding the tools to uncover updated information in real time is certainly valuable to a career that demands constant awareness and knowledge of many different industries. From the media's point of view, a job as an editor, journalist, or producer is tough enough without giving up time to correspond with public relations people who are not familiar with their publications. Media people need to work with knowledgeable professionals who understand their needs and the needs of a media outlet, and the feedback from journalists on this topic is not good (see the "Interviews" section on page 47 of this chapter). They continually complain about PR people who don't know the frequency of their publications or the lead times for story development, and don't have a basic understanding of whether a publication is targeted at consumers or a business-to-business audience.

What exactly should today's PR professional be doing? The rules of etiquette for dealing with the media are probably not much different than they were decades ago. These are the basics:

- Know when journalists are on deadline and don't reach out to them at this time.
- Understand the journalist's publication (circulation, breakdown of departments, target audience, etc.).
- Realize that journalists are looking for information that is relevant to their stories; take the time to research their writing style and trends that interest them.
- Read a journalist's column or past articles to get a feel for his or her interests.
- Look up a journalist's background; dig a little deeper into his or her hobbies and personal information, if possible.
- Identify the manners in which the journalist wants to be contacted.

MEDIA WEB SITES

What has changed in the past decade is your ability to use the Internet to gather this type of information. The place to start is with the Web sites of the publications themselves.

Many publications have recognized the efficiencies involved in making sure that PR people do not waste reporters' time with misplaced pitches, so they've placed special instructions on their Web sites for PR professionals. *InternetWeek*, which CMP Media shut down in 2002, had an online guide called "Rules of Engagement" that provided a list of reporters and their beats and a brief lesson on the publication's mission and its readership, as well as its policies concerning exclusives, embargoes, and vendor-written stories. (The guide was still online the last time we checked at *internetweek.com/pr*) Many other publications, such as *IndustryWeek* and *Medical Economics* offer similar information in the "About Us" or "Contact Us" sections of their Web sites. A few others, such as *BusinessWeek* and *ComputerWorld*, simply offer updated mastheads online, which provide e-mail links for staff writers.

The Web sites of publications can also be helpful in determining who at the publication has written most recently about your client or its industry. Many sites include archives of back issues, which you can search to determine what the publication has written about digital cameras or Nikon, for example. If you've already identified a writer to pitch, it is often possible to do a search for that person's last name to determine what he or she has been up to recently.

Finally, a growing number of news organizations—especially in the trade press—are urging their reporters to be more accessible to readers and are trying to raise the profile of their publications by having their reporters featured as experts in the mainstream media. These two goals have led magazines to publish biographies of their editors online, which can sometimes be helpful to PR people who are preparing pitches. The online bio of Lew McCreary of *CIO Magazine*, for example, includes the names of his two novels. An enterprising PR person might win favor with McCreary by taking the names of his novels to the Amazon.com site, where it is possible to read excerpts of his latest book and learn that it was made into a Hollywood movie.

THIRD-PARTY RESOURCES

Of course, every publication you want to pitch is not going to offer help on its Web site. For this reason, there are numerous third-party sources of data on the Internet that can help you research publications and journalists. If you were to type into a Yahoo! search engine "Online PR Resources," approximately 142,000 Web pages would be available to peruse. Similarly, an MSN.com search for the same inquiry would reveal 231,218 possible entries.

These tremendous numbers are more overwhelming than useful, so we'll save you some time and energy with a handful of best picks and valuable resources that we've encountered. Of course, there are more but these are surely a good start:

- Bacon's Online Media Database
- Business Wire's PR Services
- ProfNet
- CyberAlert (*cyberalert.com*), eWatch (*ewatch.com*), and Burrelle's (*burrelles.com*)
- Press-Release-Writing.com newsletter, PR Fuel newsletter, and ExpertPR newsletter
- O'Dwyer's PR Daily newsletter

These resources should give you a tremendous amount of information to better prepare you to communicate with the media. Let's discuss each one with respect to its potential for researching media contacts, pitching better story angles, distributing news releases, and monitoring communication.

At the top of the list is Bacon's Online Databases for media contacts. Bacon's is an old-time PR resource that has come a long way to keep up with the needs of professionals as technology advances. The Bacon's books of the past are now available online with real-time updates (approximately 5,000 daily) and more than 500,000 journalists and media outlets for review. PR professionals not only receive contact information, but a wealth of information to aid in the relationship-building process. It's just a matter of making enough time to peruse what the online databases have to offer. The service, which is priced at approximately $3,000 for a year-long contract and an additional $300 for more than one user, allows PR people to access the following data quickly and with reasonable assurance that it is up-to-date:

- Contact information, including e-mail addresses
- General overview of a media outlet
- Pitching tips for a particular media person
- Merge list capabilities for mailings
- Editorial calendars

We've asked a few PR representatives their opinions of Bacon's online databases. After all, the senior-level professionals make the decision on the service but the account executives, assistant account executives, and interns are the individuals who have the pleasure of using the service. It's amazing that no matter how quickly users can log on to *baconsmediasource.com* and enter their password to access information, it's just never quick enough for young PR representatives. After speaking with several Generation-Y public relations people, we've come to the conclusion that for this age group, no technology will ever be considered to be in "Gen-Y time." Then, there are the members of Gen-X, who have been exposed to slower technologies and manual methods. On the contrary, they are amazed at the ability to use Bacon's for creating media lists with hundreds of journalists (using specific search criteria for better media targeting). Obviously, Gen-Y did not have the pleasure of using the *Bacon's Media Guides* of the past. In any case, other than the usual technological glitch here and there, Bacon's Online is truly an asset to a PR agency. It's simple and Bacon's aims to please all groups along the spectrum of technology adopters, with functions for the more technologically savvy and features for the less sophisticated. Most groups are consistently pleased with Bacon's service and its online interactive databases for PR media research.

Business Wire is another PR tool of monumental importance. With many wire services to choose from, we feel Business Wire stands apart from the crowd with its broad reach, reasonable pricing structure, and helpful customer service department. When a colleague of ours reached out to Business Wire because she was being criticized by a client for a news release that went over the wire, she received immediate attention from her sales representative. Initially, the woman wrote an e-mail note to her representative stating, "We've got a doubting Thomas on our hands . . . He wants to know if we used the right circuit to launch his release." She passed along the names of other news wire services that the doubting Thomas had suggested using. Within a few hours of her inquiry, the representative wrote back with a complete breakdown of the circuit that had been used, information revealing the media outlets contacted, and proof that the other wire services that the doubting Thomas had suggested actually used Business Wire as well. The woman was able to squelch the negativism from her client and Business Wire remained the company's choice for news distribution. Business Wire is known in the industry for its ability to deliver news to more news sources than any other distributor and it uses technology to remain on the leading edge of news distribution. Business Wire covers a huge range of industries and PR professionals are able to target messages to the appropriate circuits whether they are of national or regional distribution or narrowed down to high-tech, entertainment, sports, or health wires. In addition, with an online sign-up distribution system, it's simple for the PR professional to input all of the news release information and distribution instructions for Business Wire to deliver to the appropriate circuits via the Internet.

Other interesting features include the ability to add multimedia into a news release. With the Smart News release, a company can incorporate logos, video, audio, Flash materials, photos, graphics, or a slide show—certainly richer than the faxed news releases of the past. Business Wire might actually be pulling some PR agencies into the future with this service. More and more, executives are asking for graphics in news releases. One such incident occurred at Greg Manning Auction's Teletrade when it announced its PremierPlus auction. A new VP at Greg Manning, who had recently come over from Sotheby's, instructed the PR agency to put graphics in the news release because he felt trade publications used such releases as stories—headlines, graphics, and all. After some initial hesitation, the executive vice president at the PR firm gave the word: "If our client wants graphics in the release (as long as the file is not too heavy to send via e-mail) then don't worry about it. Don't think about what you used to do—this is how we're going to do it today!"

Another valuable tool for PR professionals is ProfNet, Inc., a subsidiary of PR Newswire. ProfNet is used by both PR people and the media as a place where journalists and PR professionals can collaborate and share expert resources in real time. Of the many useful features on ProfNet, one of the most helpful is the ability to receive e-mails of journalists' queries, and reach out to journalists with your clients' expertise to answer questions for their stories. These queries are e-mailed up to four times a day in North America and two times a day in Europe. PR professionals also have access to an experts database in which they can list their clients' profiles for journalists to peruse when searching for expert commentary for their stories. The objective of ProfNet is to give journalists the ability to reach qualified individuals quickly and conveniently. The service goes so far as to instruct experts on the netiquette of contacting journalists. ProfNet states that a three-paragraph response to the journalist's inquiry works best. The fist paragraph, of course, is the client's contact information. The second paragraph is composed of the expert's credentials and the last paragraph gives a summary of the expert's thoughts on the subject queried.

Anyone concerned about what is being written online or in print about their clients really needs to subscribe to an online clipping service offered by the likes of CyberAlert, eWatch, or Burrelle's. We talk in greater detail in Chapter 10 about how these services work, but in short, they are generally affordable at a few hundred dollars a month and extremely important to PR people who are trying to determine who is writing about their clients and their clients' competitors. Electronic clippings, which are delivered much more rapidly than old-fashioned paper clippings, can be even more valuable than online media guides because they enable PR people to see for themselves the types of articles that a Web site or publication covers and the attitudes and opinions that writers might reveal in their articles.

If you are not planning to use paid Internet services for online databases, lead generation, distribution, or monitoring services, the Internet is also a fantastic source of free industry knowledge that can help you refine your practices. Registering for complimentary newsletters is an easy way to gain insight on topics such as these:

- News release writing tips
- Media contacts
- Pitching ideas and guidelines
- New online PR techniques
- Methods to integrate online and offline PR programs
- PR opportunities for saturated markets
- Trend watching and monitoring of competition

Of the many newsletters (and there are an abundance that can show up in your mailbox), some of the tried-and-true sources that have survived the dot-com collapse are PR Newswire's newsletter (*press-release-writing.com*), PR Fuel of eReleases (*ereleases.com*), and MediaMap's ExpertPR Newsletter (*mediamap.com/expertpr/default.htm*).

Starting with Press-Release-Writing.com, how much can you write about a news release in a newsletter? Plenty. This free newsletter gives the finer details of news release writing and often is a good reminder of what we sometimes forget as we advance in our careers and get caught up in the daily chaos of our jobs. However, Press-Release-Writing.com always makes us feel that what we do is important and it must be carefully developed. It's more than just writing a news release in the right format and Associated Press (AP) style. It's about those overlooked techniques that we can incorporate into our writing to get better responses. For instance, the newsletter on August 15, 2001, contained a feature article titled, "Name-Dropping Adds Familiarity, Credibility to a Press Release," which reminded us of a simple but often overlooked technique that can easily be incorporated into a release. As long as it's legitimate name dropping of Fortune 500 executives or celebrities, it is acceptable; better yet, put it in the headline.

A second favorite newsletter is eRelease's PR Fuel. Its August 8, 2001, issue, called "Five Steps to a Newsworthy Non-Profit," caused three PR professionals from the same agency to e-mail one another with variations of the same message: "Good stuff, check this out," "Definitely worth reading," and "Did you see this?" Typical of this newsletter is its ability to get PR professionals to understand their audiences' needs and to put themselves in the reader's shoes, which further enforces the need to constantly do your research homework. A favorite PR Fuel newsletter focused on creating PR opportunity when there's very little opportunity available to the naked eye. Again, this is a useful tool to make you think differently about your clients and the publicity they receive. This article covered some interesting techniques focusing on the Internet's ability to quickly reach the right media outlet. This included everything from "hot topic" lists accompanied by a short note to a journalist and op-ed articles, to registering for speaking opportunities online, and perfecting homegrown media databases by continually researching the Web sites of media outlets.

ExpertPR, the free publication of MediaMap is also at the top of the list of well-known online newsletters. MediaMap publishes many articles, usually focusing on current events and the views of PR professionals in the news. Especially valuable are the articles that look at the PR industry from the perspective of its clients. The August 23, 2001 issue of ExpertPR, for example, included an article titled "Leaders Cite Tight Budgets, Keep PR Work In-House." It explained, without sugarcoating, the difficulties facing PR agencies in a tough economy and chronicled the areas in which business executives said the PR industry needed to improve.

The last newsletter worth mentioning is *O'Dwyer's PR Daily* online (*odwyerpr.com*). This resource is established, well known, and trusted by industry professionals. Jack O'Dwyer is one of the true PR gurus and he has put most of his newsletters on the Web. The site is an excellent resource for professionals to see what's going on inside the PR industry. In addition, O'Dwyer's allows professionals to access articles and information on the media. It's often said that, "Anyone who is anyone is written about in Jack O'Dwyer's newsletter."

As you can see, the abundance of useful resources available on the Internet leaves very little room for excuses for not doing your homework. However, as we close this chapter, we feel the need to reiterate a point made at the start of this chapter: PR professionals must still have the basic skills necessary to use the intelligence they gather on the Web to cultivate the strong relationships with the press that will ultimately lead to editorial placements.

One PR veteran of more than 25 years Andrew Edson, president of the New York PR firm Andrew Edson & Associates, observes how he has seen technologies from the telex to the fax machine to the Internet change the PR industry. The Internet has been the most revolutionary, he says, noting the tremendous popularity of e-mail due to its speed. Online newswires like Business Wire and PR Newswire have also changed the business with their ability to meet the needs of audiences who have become more particular about how they receive their news and information, Edson says.

However, Edson believes the Internet will still never replace the relationships of the past when PR people used to have more face-to-face interactions with journalists over lunch or for coffee breaks. Even news conferences are dwindling, he notes, given that corporate announcements can roll out over the Internet wire or be Webcast for audience participation.

"Today is a different world," Edson acknowledges, still holding fast to his belief that PR people must turn away from their computer keyboards with the results of their research and then talk to people to validate their results before rolling out any communication.

MEDIA INTERVIEWS: WHAT THE REPORTERS SAY

The best way to determine if public relations professionals are using the Internet to educate themselves better about publications and about journalists is to ask the journalists. We went to a number of reporters and editors employed by a range of organizations—from prominent print publications like *The New York Times* to newer, Web-based journals—and asked, "Are things getting better?" Their resounding answer: No. The journalists said that the large majority of PR professionals are failing to take advantage of the Internet to work more wisely.

How can the journalists be so sure? Just look at their overstuffed e-mail inboxes. PR practitioners, by and large, are not using the information available on the Net to winnow out those reporters who would be inappropriate for a particular pitch. Instead, the cost efficiencies of e-mail seem to encourage PR people to spread their pitches widely, further inflaming the anger of journalists.

Reporters say the situation was at its worst during the height of the dot-com frenzy. They say it was typical for PR people representing Internet companies to display little familiarity with the publication or Web site they were contacting and often little familiarity with their own clients. It seemed to many reporters that PR firms were taking on new clients quickly and assigning inexperienced workers to call on as many news organizations as possible, even if the callers were incapable of answering simple questions about the client's business model or history. "One of the worst examples was PR people calling and just reading press releases," recalls Anna Maria Virzi, managing editor of Ziff-Davis's *Baseline* magazine, who held senior positions with *Internet World* magazine and Forbes.com during the Internet's craziest days. "Everyone was pitching everybody," she adds. "It was just insanity."

Those representing traditional "old economy" companies also seemed oblivious to online resources like magazine Web sites that could help them target their pitches more accurately. "PR people, like salespeople, are more likely to consult their contact management software or personal files than do 'research' on the Web," says Ellis Booker, editor of Crain's *BtoB* magazine. "They don't read our publications—unless, maybe, their client is featured in one story." Booker says he's been particularly irritated by the pitches related to business-to-consumer news that are inappropriate for the business-to-business scope of his magazine, which he says should be apparent by its name.

In defense of PR practitioners, many journalists admit that the rise of the Internet as a news vehicle, the subsequent economic hardships caused by the demise of dot-coms, and the overall recession have probably made it hard for many PR professionals to keep up with the way media organizations are positioning themselves. With more news delivered online, print publications have struggled to determine what to cover on their Web sites versus what to feature on paper. Declining revenues have meant repositionings as publications churn out fewer issues per year and try to target those niches where they see the most growth potential. All the repositioning has often been accompanied by employee turnover and downsizing. Many news organizations have tried to keep PR people apprised of their changes by posting explanations online. *Internet Week*, a CMP Media trade publication that ceased publishing in 2002, was a good example of a publication that devoted a portion of its Web site to explaining its deadlines, its beats, and its policies concerning embargoes and exclusives.

Dave Joachim, *Internet Week's* former senior managing editor, says the "Rules of Engagement" published on the site worked hand-in-hand with the voice-mail messages of editorial employees, which directed callers to check out the Web site. "Each of us got so many calls simply asking who covered X, Y, or Z," Joachim says in recalling the motivation for the Web page. "We thought that if we could cut down that volume 10 percent, we could each steal back several hours per month."

Putting the information online "wasn't a ton of effort," says Joachim, who notes that continuing maintenance was necessary for just the beat list, which changed with employee turnover. He says he's not sure the initiative resulted in hours saved for all of *Internet Week's* reporters, but it was clear to him that a lot of PR professionals perused the Web pages before calling.

MarketingSherpa.com, a Web site devoted to articles about marketing trends, also has a site feature called "PR People: How to get coverage for your clients through us," but publisher Anne Holland says she still hears from numerous PR people who haven't tried to familiarize themselves with her site and its mission. "I still get countless personal pitches from PR people who are hawking technology," she says, noting her site's clearly stated focus on marketing. "Sometimes when I'm caffeinated and have a few extra minutes to burn I e-mail them back saying 'We don't cover tech. Just marketing, marketing, marketing.' If they surfed my site for 15 seconds, or bothered to read our 'for PR people' section they would have known that."

Similarly, Holland says, PR people fail to recognize her site's emphasis on interviews and case studies. "I also get endless news releases, when I don't cover news at all," she complains. "I figure some are folks just trying to keep their name in front of me, which is okay. But the ones who follow-up in e-mail or phone calls I snap at. Honestly, why waste my time when you can see for yourself that I don't carry news?"

Holland and some of her colleagues are hopeful that PR people will soon seize the Internet's power to deliver only those pitches that are relevant to a particular media organization. She says she's seen more personalized pitches since the economy slowed down, a development that she suggests could be due to the fact that PR agencies are getting to know their clients better and the reporters that follow them. An alternative explanation, she suggests, is that the laziest, least competent PR people have been laid off.

Baseline's Virzi is less certain there's been much improvement even in slower economic times. "People still aren't doing their homework," she says, noting *Baseline*'s focus not on technology, but on the results and return on investment of technology projects. "All those people pitching new technology, for the most part, are wasting my time," she says.

Lisa Guernsey, a technology reporter for the Circuits section of *The New York Times*, estimates that the lean economy may have helped the percentage of useful e-mail pitches rise to 20 percent, up from 10 percent in the past. "What's related to smarter PR and what's related to having just less money to throw around?" she asks. "There's still this flurry of uselessness that's out there."

Holland, of MarketingSherpa.com, advises PR people who are making the effort to personalize and target pitches to use the subject line wisely to tell journalists what's in the e-mail. "A subject line reading 'Press Release From' or 'News From' or some other ultra-dull subject won't stand out in my clogged inbox," she says. Something like "P&G Case Study for MarketingSherpa" is going to do a much better job of telling her about the contents and of indicating that the PR person has made an effort to target the release, she says.

Booker of *BtoB* notes, however, that the personalization has to be real and not something that is accomplished with a merge command that just inserts the recipient's name in the subject line. "If it's a carpet-bomb press release, why make it personal?" he asks.

Guernsey, at *The New York Times,* recalls an e-mail from the once high-flying online retailer eToys that cut through the e-mail clutter and captured her attention. She credits Jonathan Cutler, a former manager of communications at eToys, with acknowledging in the first sentences that he was aware that *The Times* was getting lots of pitches from online retailers in advance of the upcoming holiday season. He then quickly pointed out that eToys had hired a new logistics officer to address the fulfillment problems that had been a concern for so many Internet merchants. "I definitely took the bait on that one," says Guernsey, who subsequently accepted Cutler's invitation to visit an eToys distribution center in Blairs, Virginia. The result was a story, sidebar, and photo that were featured prominently in *The Times* on December 7, 2000.

Cutler, who is now a vice president of Porter Novelli, recalls that his pitch was to give the media a chance to catch a rare glimpse behind the scenes of "online toyland" during the holiday season, but the hiring of the logistics officer gave him a newsy angle and helped attract attention beyond *The Times* at NBC, CBS, and elsewhere. He recalled the pitch in the following e-mail he sent us:

> I had been tracking Lisa Guernsey's stories for more than six months. Obviously the section lent itself well to eToys, a rising star of the Internet, but one couldn't just pitch the story of an online retailer. Besides, there were already other reporters at the *NYT* that covered eToys from a strictly business perspective. I was looking to demonstrate both the parents' appeal of our business and how we were helping to transform the way people live and work (by shopping online for kids' toys, something that traditionally was an often overwhelming and laborious process in the brick-and-mortar world). So, the pitch I used to approach the *NYT* tapped into both what Circuits covered, what Lisa had been writing about, and what was timely and relevant overall. The pitch: meet the Millennium Santa and take a peek into his new age Santa's workshop; meet the digital elves and see how eToys was going to deliver Christmas, Chanukah, and Kwanza to tens of thousands of American children.
>
> The *NYT* broke this story, but many print publications soon followed with scaled-down versions of the piece. The *NYT* story also helped secure a series of broadcast pieces along the same theme, including a feature piece on *NBC Nightly News* and *CBS This Morning*. Overall, we were very successful in generating widespread stories in all mediums (print, broadcast, and online) and were able to develop meaningful and relevant story angles that appealed to both the reporter and ultimately the public.

It is essential to know both the publication inside and out, and what the reporter you are pitching covers. The last thing you want to do is lose the interest of a reporter because you didn't take the time to understand their particular beat and track past articles they have written. The Internet is one way to help focus your pitch. It provides an accessible means by which to research a publication and those that write for it. It also provides an unlimited pool from which to do research on trends and other factors that may play into your pitch.

Certain rules that must always be followed when approaching the media with a story would include first and foremost knowing the publication and understanding the writing style of the specific reporter you are pitching. You can't just send a press release or make a phone call without connecting the dots. The story must have relevance, be timely, and most of all tap into either an existing trend or help identify an emerging one. It is important to be well versed with both your subject (whether it is a product, service, or executive) and equally as informed with the media outlet. Always be concise in your pitch and demonstrate that your story idea is both topical and meaningful.

Virzi, of *Baseline* magazine, says the most effective PR professionals are the ones who use the Internet to keep up with what publications are covering and what beats staff members have and then keep good notes on whether the reporters prefer e-mail or phone calls and whether they are early birds like herself who prefer calls at 8 a.m., or late risers who prefer to take calls after lunch. "You've really got to know the likes and dislikes of people," she says.

However, PR people who become too proficient at keeping tabs on journalists need to watch out for the occasional backlash from writers who find the practice a little spooky. A lot of reporters who enjoy covering newsmakers are private people who don't necessarily like having the spotlight on themselves. Whereas some might respond well to a PR person who has investigated where they went to college or who their favorite sports teams are, others might be put off by tactics that may view as transparent and manipulative.

Lisa DiCarlo, a senior editor for Forbes.com and a veteran of *PCWeek*, is among those who is uncomfortable with some of the information being collected by PR professionals. She recalls seeing the dossier kept on her by a large computer maker. She says she wasn't bothered by the records the company kept of stories she had written or by the company's conclusions about the "tone" of her articles. What made her uneasy, she says, was an attempt by the company to decipher her nonverbal communications during an in-person interview. In her case, the PR people for the computer company observed that she "doesn't divert her eyes from the executive to write in the notepad" and advised executives who might be interviewed by her that this was "an intimidation tactic on my part," she says.

DiCarlo says more research into what she covers and how she covers it could very well be the solution for ending the tide of misdirected e-mail pitches that overwhelms her and her colleagues in journalism. "But examining the personal interviewing styles was creepy." ■

5. THE NEED FOR CONTINUOUS RESEARCH

> Online tools can help you collect the data you need about customers' needs.
> Log software helps you analyze where your site visitors are going.
> Surveys enable you to ask people about what they are seeking.

Now that you're up to speed on how to keep up with journalists of the Internet era, remember that the Internet has created a whole new audience for PR professionals to worry about. As we've pointed out earlier, the public now has new access to the PR messages and brand image that you are helping your clients create online. We talked in Chapter 2 about the secondary research indicating the continued rapid growth of Internet use and the growth in previously underrepresented demographic segments, such as women and older Americans. We discussed in Chapter 3 the need for PR and marketing professionals to conduct primary research to understand the needs that consumers are seeking to satisfy and the product benefits that clients should strive to offer.

In this chapter, we discuss some of the tools you can use to collect this information from your online visitors. The tools range from Internet log and analysis software, which can be licensed or subscribed to as a service, all the way up to third-party vendors that can help you in conducting surveys or focus groups of your online visitors.

This is research that clients should conduct for reasons that go far beyond public relations. Finding out who is visiting a Web site, for what purpose, at what times, and for how long are all important factors in crafting the client's image, but also in determining marketing and product development strategies, and in answering technical questions about the expected burden on Web site servers. Therefore, PR professionals should look to other departments of a client's business to build support for (and share the costs of) the type of primary research we propose here.

One cost-effective place to start with your research is with the log software that records activity on a Web site. You'll probably find this software already installed on your Web servers to aid technical professionals in keeping the site online and secure, but this software can also provide a wealth of information for PR people and marketers eager to find out about Web site visitors. The software is available from a variety of vendors, including market leader WebTrends, a formerly independent company that is now part of NetIQ Corp. of San Jose, California.

WebTrends can tell you, for example, the most frequently requested Web pages on a client's site. Are visitors interested in the online press releases you've posted? If so, are they more interested in the ones related to new products or the ones concerning quarterly earnings? The software can also tell you if visitors are coming back repeatedly and the average amount of time they're spending on the site. Is it a quick drop-by or are they doing some serious research requiring a bit of time and involving lots of page views? Are people making most of their visits during business hours when they might be researching potential purchases or partnerships or are they coming on weekends or at night when they might be using their own time to check out stock tips?

Log software can be especially helpful if your client is operating a closed Web site in which customers and business partners are given IDs and passwords to access information. In such cases, it is possible to determine how many times a particular user logs in and what pages that user views. Jeff Seacrist, group product manager for WebTrends, says it might be possible to link what you know about a customer's surfing habits to offline data about his or her buying history to customize the Web experience so that the customer is offered deals on merchandise that is most appropriate for that person. "It's important for any site doing this to have a well-thought-through privacy policy," he adds, noting the sensitivity many people have to the way in which personal data is handled. "The policy needs to say what they do and they need to do what they say."

In cases where people are not logging into a closed site, it is still possible to glean information about users. A bit of code known as a *cookie* can unobtrusively be attached to a user's browser software to identify whether the user is a first-timer or a returning visitor. Log software also records the Internet Protocol (IP) address of visitors, so it is possible to determine how many people are entering a client's site via Internet connections at universities (*.edu* addresses), military organizations (*.mil* addresses), or commercial entities (*.com* addresses). These IP addresses can also indicate the scope of international interest in your client's Web site, as computers outside the United States often have Internet addresses ending with a country-specific suffix, such as .uk for the United Kingdom or .jp for Japan. Some software vendors also claim to be able to identify the states and cities of Internet visitors based on their IP addresses, but such claims are a little shaky in our view. The 35 million people logging on through AOL may be routed through servers at the company's Virginia headquarters, but they are not all Virginians. Seacrist of WebTrends acknowledges such problems, but says IP addresses still hold value for Web site operators. "If you know the majority of your visitors come from warmer climates, you don't show your parkas on the home page," he says.

Another valuable source of information available from Web site logs is the data about where visitors from your site were before they came to your site. This could tell you which business partner is passing the most traffic to you. It can also tell you which search engine is frequently used to find your site. Links from search engines are also valuable because the search phrase is captured in the referral from the search engine. Which of your client's products are people searching for? Which segments of your client's business are the subject of most searches? Once you know the phrases people are searching, you can replicate the searches and see where your client is positioned on the results list vis à vis its competitors.

Finally, Seacrist of WebTrends points to the entry point as another piece of data captured in Web logs that could be attractive to marketers and PR people concerned about putting a client's best foot forward. Log software generally tells you which door visitors are coming through when they come to a site. Are they hitting the home page or being ushered by a search engine to a certain product page inside the site? If it's the latter, then you must make sure the product pages provide easy access to the full realm of information about the company. Having data about the entry points also enables you to determine the response rates to particular press releases or advertisements. You can incorporate a unique Uniform Resource Locator (URL) in the release or ad for a particular product and then use log software to determine how many people come through that door. The software can also tell you what percentage of the people who come through that door ultimately make an online purchase and what percentage read multiple pages on your site and therefore could be considered good prospective customers.

Of course, looking at records of site visits and inferring what people are doing online is an imperfect science. This has left the door open for a variety of researchers who will actually communicate with Internet users to find out what they are doing and what they have to say about various sites. "We've got the why behind what happens with Web logs," says Janice Caston, director of marketing for Greenfield Online of Wilton, Connecticut, one of several firms specializing in online market research. "You could be missing the boat with Web logs because you're really not understanding your users," she says.

Greenfield Online offers sites a variety of services for finding out about their visitors. A low-end service called Quick-Take is intended to help them do a cheap, quick evaluation of their users on their own. Another service uses questionnaires to help sites find out about the demographics of their users and their users' opinions of the site's aesthetic appeal and usability. A third service, called WebSuite, involves an ongoing evaluation of users so that a site can see how visitors respond to changes in the site or to various promotions. Finally, Greenfield Online also maintains a panel of consumers that it can call on to do a competitive analysis of sites in a given industry. Panel members visit the client's site and the sites of his or her competitors and then answer a series of questions about the sites. Such comparisons can produce a wealth of information about which Web features are attracting the most attention in a particular demographic group.

Greenfield's Caston says a key to getting site users to respond to surveys is to keep surveys short. A survey done of Greenfield Online panel members can be longer, sometimes as long as 40 questions, because these people have signed up to participate in research studies over time. However, incentives are still often necessary, Caston notes, and rewards need to be viewed as attainable if large numbers of people are going to take the time to respond. Greenfield Online has learned that awarding respondents a chance in a $5,000 raffle is less effective, she says, than entering them in a smaller $50 raffle that boasts a much better chance of winning.

Survey.com also uses a panel of online users to conduct market research. The company, which is profiled in an interview on page 61 of this chapter, says the breadth of its ePanel enables it to gather feedback from particular subgroups, such as IT decision makers, home computer buyers, or avid video gamers. Its questionnaires are intended to collect data on a variety of important topics ranging from brand perception to customer needs and satisfaction to product intelligence.

Admittedly, working with an e-marketing specialist is not cheap. Customers of Greenfield Online, Surveys.com, and the like can expect to pay upwards of $10,000 for any of their customized services. Web log software, as noted earlier, is usually a cheaper, less comprehensive solution. A middle-ground answer to your need for information about your online users might be to conduct surveys on your own.

Surveys can be developed in-house fairly simply by using Hypertext Markup Language (HTML) forms that dump responses into a database that can be analyzed with Microsoft Excel or another spreadsheet program. Vinny Cozzi, a Web developer at PFS Marketwyse, says surveys can be placed on a Web site or e-mailed to online customers. The best response rate is usually achieved by putting a short survey of one or two questions on the home page. "It's right there in front of you when you come to that home page," he notes. An e-mailed survey usually requires the recipient to follow a link to a Web page, which requires more effort than a lot of people are willing to give.

Not only should the questionnaire be brief, but the questions themselves must each be short, Cozzi says. Yes-or-no questions can tell you which products the respondent owns and a multiple-choice question can ask the user where he or she bought the product, he says. The answers can tell marketers a lot about the site's visitors, he says, including whether they buy online or offline and whether they're buying from an East Coast, West Coast, or Midwestern retailer. Satisfaction with a site or with a particular product can also be measured quickly on a scale of 1 to 10, Cozzi notes. Similar questions could be posted in an online pressroom, for example, to determine what percentages of visitors are from daily newspapers, trade press, radio, TV, Web sites, and so forth.

"You try to make it as easy as possible," Cozzi says, noting the need to get as many responses as possible. He says such questionnaires can be developed in as little as one day or as many as two weeks. Those requiring the most time are usually the ones in which the client desires a high level of detail about user demographics, product preferences, and other factors— all of which need to be built into the reporting system for the questionnaire.

Sites unable to devote their own resources to designing and developing questionnaires and reporting systems can also choose among a variety of software packages intended to make it easy to post surveys or polls. The packages range from freeware like PollCat Polls to hosted services like Uptilt's Polling Engine. Active Websurvey is one poll-making software from Webintel.net, which is available through a three-month subscription for $166 or by license for $499 a year. It enables users to develop their own surveys, which are hosted on Active Websurvey's servers. Users are provided with passwords for accessing reports and charts on Active Websurvey's servers.

Now that you've accumulated all of this research, let's turn our attention to how you can use it. The opening chapters of this book have been intended to help you understand the needs and online behaviors of the reporters and general public who are interacting with your client. Part II of this book commences with the next chapter, as we discuss the strategies and tools to be used in communicating your client's story in the Internet age.

INTERVIEW WITH MICHAEL BACH, CEO AND FOUNDER OF SURVEY.COM

What better method than online research to deliver mission-critical information? Survey.com has been identifying and delivering this type of research to its clients since 1994, when the company was founded by its CEO Michael Bach. Although Survey.com is a full-service market research company, its expertise lies in online research, including the development of Web evaluation surveys, the recruitment and set-up of e-panels, and the execution of Web-based surveys and e-polling. What should be of particular interest to PR professionals is Survey.com's staff of trained professionals and their knowledge and experience with public relations research.

Bach discussed with us how Survey.com strives to provide public relations professionals with credible information regarding audience attitudes, perceptions, and beliefs. "Our clients use Survey.com because they know that data published regarding opinions moves opinions," he says. "We don't always find the information that our clients expect to hear, but provide them with the accurate findings that they need to be aware of when it comes to changing opinions of audiences online." Bach also says that Survey.com's ability to compile opinions from a large pool of survey respondents (15 million consumers) aids PR professionals by helping them get data they need to support the messages they are putting out in news releases.

According to Bach, the key benefits to using online research are two-fold. PR professionals find benefit in Survey.com when they are seeking an independent study or statistics that support a company's communication. Bach, in discussing PR research, also knows that PR professionals look to reputable firms for their research (i.e., Gallup Polls have the name and reputation for population surveys). He also realizes that Survey.com must provide extremely targeted research, and be sensitive to newsworthy, credible statistics, avoiding the hype that has been all too often displayed on the Internet. Bach feels that his company has advanced in the past 10 years to the point of doing "incredibly targeted research," which has led to relationships with medium- to large-sized customers including eBay, IBM, the U.S. Navy, Cisco Systems, and Ford Motor Company.

The scope of Survey.com's research ranges from internal to external PR research. With many companies looking inward and re-evaluating market positions, internal, message-oriented PR has moved to the forefront. In addition, companies call on Survey.com to find out what employees are thinking with respect to communication programs. This helps senior-level executives with internal communication to guide the future direction of the company. Message-oriented PR is also popular with external audiences. Companies often ask Survey.com for answers to many popular online research questions, such as, "We'd like to know what our audiences think about the company?" and "Will our target audience even know who we are?"

Bach says Survey.com can answer such questions and offers benefits in other areas, such as these:

- **Time:** It's much faster to complete surveys using the Internet. A survey that might have taken a week to implement now takes a day and research that quite possibly took several weeks only takes one week.

- **Cost:** Online research is less expensive. A few years ago, a budget of $50,000 would not extend a company's research into other countries.

Today, online research enables this type of budget to delve into international territories—perhaps as many as five countries—complete with reported translations.

There are always issues concerning whether or not survey research online is representative of the population. Bach explains that Survey.com's sampling techniques range from probability through expert and snowballing methods. Bach points out that the survey world is broken into two spheres—those who take surveys and those who do not. Faced with the challenge that some online visitors will not donate their time or attention to a survey, Bach knows that Survey.com needs a variety of effective solicitation methods (based on incentives for better response). These methods include the following:

- Surveys via e-mail with the ability for participants to click on a dynamic URL that recognizes who they are and which survey they should complete.

- Surveys via pop-up windows, which are used for Web evaluation and analysis. A Web site pop-up survey can be coded so that a random sample is achieved; for instance every hundredth or every tenth visitor sees the pop-up box survey.

- Direct mail cards and advertising invite participants to log onto a Web site to complete a survey.

- Even telephone solicitation coaxes people to log on to the Internet to complete a questionnaire.

Of course, there are rewards for participation. Survey.com uses an incentive-based model—not to be confused with "paid responses." Most incentives are contest based when dealing with consumers. However, the business-to-business respondents participate with Survey.com for the purpose of getting valuable input to major manufacturers. Survey.com does not "overincent" for fear that completing surveys will become mercenary work. As a result, the company steers clear of overusing panelist participants for e-panels. According to Bach, many companies are hurt by oversurveying or oversampling of their participants on the Internet. Survey.com looks to newer audiences and fresh opinions. Bach feels that with growing numbers of people on the Internet and a wider range of demographics, finding fresh opinions is far less difficult than it was in the earlier years of online research.

Bach's final thoughts were that the Internet is becoming increasingly popular and as a result gathering data is easier and more accurate. Online research is advancing quickly. Bach sees more access points and far more interaction with research respondents. "Research online is not a revolution, it's an evolution," he says. He stresses that as long as professionals understand the rules, restrictions, and guidelines, companies such as Survey.com will find success. In fact, Survey.com has found success with a wide range of clients who compliment the company for its responsiveness, customer satisfaction, and knowledge about the type of research that is necessary for PR professionals. The fact that 90 percent of his clients come back for more online research speaks for itself. ∎

II

Putting the Tools to Work

6 BUILDING YOUR ONLINE NEWSROOM

➤ Journalists expect companies to have easily accessible online newsrooms.
➤ Online newsrooms free PR people from paper shuffling so they can think more about strategy.
➤ Don't hide behind your online newsroom because the human touch is still important.

Now you're ready to get down to the business of using the Internet for public relations.

We've sensitized you to the need to understand the different technology comfort levels of reporters and consumers. We've talked about the need to position your client as a solution to a need. We've told you where to get secondary information about Internet users and clued you in about Internet tools and services that can help you target the appropriate journalists and learn about the interests of your client's Web visitors.

Now it's time to talk about how you put all of this information to work. In this chapter we talk in greater detail about how your approach to the news media has to evolve with the changing times. We'll hear firsthand from reporters about how their work styles have changed because of the Internet and why they consider your company or your clients to be technologically backwards and PR-challenged if they don't, at the least, have an online newsroom full of up-to-date documents. In subsequent chapters, we provide our advice on the best ways to use other tools such as e-mail, newsletters, and Webcasts.

A NEW WORLD

It's no secret that technological advancements have changed the journalism world dramatically in the last 30 years. The switch from typewriters to computers speeded up the production process and bought journalists more time to complete their stories. Similarly, the advent of cold type technology saved lots of time because it eliminated the need to set hot type. However, all of those changes cannot compare to what the Internet has already done for journalism and will do in the coming years as more reporters recognize what is available to them.

The modernization of production processes might have bought reporters and editors enough extra time to polish the writing of a newspaper or magazine article, to try the fourth version of a headline, or even to swap out a story at the last minute for breaking news. Those are all important improvements. However, the Internet goes far beyond any of that because it improves not only the timeliness but also the quality of the journalistic product. Today's journalists have quick and easy access to databases of past articles, huge directories of people and companies, every financial report filed with the Securities and Exchange Commission (SEC), and large archives of reports from other government agencies, analyst organizations, and think tanks. The old practice of reporting only the facts of an event or announcement and leaving much of the background and analyses for a "second-day story" has been thrown out the window because it is now possible to provide the reader with large amounts of background data and context in a first-day story.

A reporter at *The Smalltown Gazette* in the Midwest who is writing about the appointment of a new president at Smalltown

University, for example, does not need to report primarily what the college has said about the president's background. A quick search on a search engine such as Google (*google.com*) would probably reveal lots of information about the college where the person has been working previously and how it compares to Smalltown Univeristy in terms of size and types of courses offered. That search might also reveal newspaper articles about the new president—including everything from routine coverage of past graduations to more interesting stories about clashes with the faculty and student groups at the person's former campus. Given that a lot of academic journals are online, it might also be possible to find reviews of books or articles the new president has written in a particular academic field, which should produce a path to the reviewers themselves, who might be willing to be interviewed for the reporter's article. Suddenly, a few keystrokes and mouse clicks have turned what would have been a press release story and photo a few years ago into a much richer report for the reader.

Similarly, an Internet-savvy reporter at *The Smalltown Gazette* is also much better equipped to report on the acquisition of the local Smalltown Factory by Multinational Conglomerate Corp. (MCC). It is no longer necessary to request a press kit from MCC's headquarters in London or to rely on a PR person to fax over backgrounders. MCC's Web site probably offers a full pressroom, complete with biographies and downloadable photographs of the company's executives and comprehensive descriptions of the company's various product lines. A quick search on Yahoo! Finance tells the reporter that the company's stock is near its 52-week low and reveals that the most recent headlines have been about MCC's need to improve its margins. Suddenly, the story has gone beyond the news of the factory's acquisition to a deeper look at MCC's motivations for the deal. Is this a troubled company drawn to Smalltown to cut labor costs? What does that mean for local workers? A quick check of Hoover's Online (*hoovers.com*) or CBS MarketWatch (*cbs.marketwatch.com*) reveals the names of the analysts who might comment on why they think MCC is coming to Smalltown. In the space of an hour, the *Gazette* reporter is on to a story that's probably less pleasing to the Smalltown Chamber of Commerce, but more informative for readers.

One element missing from both of these hypothetical scenarios is any mention of PR professionals. To be fair, we should acknowledge the role of the PR people in issuing press releases about the new president and the factory acquisition. We should also assume that the PR person was involved in making sure that the reporter for the *Gazette* got an interview in person or on the phone with the new college president and an MCC executive to get some colorful quotes. However, the PR person is clearly no longer holding all the cards because the Internet is an easily accessible treasure of information. The PR people at Smalltown University and MCC are left hoping that they've done their best to put their messages out on the Internet and that they've done a solid enough job of relationship building so that the *Gazette* reporter will call them for their comments and input as the story becomes richer and possibly less flattering.

IMPERATIVE #1:
A GOOD ONLINE PRESSROOM

This changing dynamic between reporters and PR folks is why it is extremely important for PR professionals to think proactively about what they are going to provide in online pressrooms. Reporters of the 21st Century expect to be able to help themselves to the information that they need and are likely to think of a company as backwards or archaic if its Web site does not have a full pressroom. "There's a real autonomy now in terms of journalism," says journalism professor Dianne Lynch of St. Michael's College in Vermont, who suggests that the Internet has changed journalism more dramatically than many PR people have recognized. (For more on Lynch's views, see the "Journalist Interview" section on page 86 of this chapter.)

It is not surprising that technology companies that were the first to climb on the Internet bandwagon and that work with the most technically savvy journalists have been the pioneers in development of online pressrooms. Microsoft, IBM, and Sun Microsystems offer examples of the types of media centers that PR professionals should aspire to create for their clients.

Microsoft's PressPass section, for example, boasts a large archive of press releases that can be browsed by month or searched by keyword. Stories published by others news organizations are included on the site, as are question-and-answer sessions that the company's public relations people have conducted with important executives. Press releases about new product announcements include links to Web pages elsewhere on the Microsoft site that provide detailed information about the company's products. Biographies are available of key Microsoft executives as well as copies of their recent speeches. The Image Gallery includes everything from assorted company and product logos to product shots to portraits of Microsoft executives—available as smaller, low-resolution images suitable for the Web or as bigger, higher resolution images suitable for print publications. Chairman Bill Gates has his own section in the PressPass area where Web users can find his biography and links to the many articles and columns he has written for *The New York Times*, *The Economist*, and other publications. Finally, Microsoft has recognized that it's impossible to anticipate and answer every question in an online document and so the contact information for the company's PR representatives is prominently featured.

Similarly, Sun Microsystems has done a comprehensive job in providing information about its people and products in its Press & Media Center. Press releases can be sorted by month or searched by keyword. A Press Kit Center offers access to collections of information put together for various product lines, for various markets such as health care, and for industry trade shows. The health-care press kit, for example, includes recent press releases related to that market as well as case studies of health-care customers, white papers related to the industry, and biographies and photos of the Sun executives responsible for that particular market. Sun's press site also includes other links to frequently requested logos and photographs. CEO Scott McNealey does not have his own elaborate site like his rival Gates, but Sun does offer downloadable photos and brief bios of him and other top decision makers at the company.

IBM, of course, cannot allow itself to be overshadowed by other blue chip technology companies. Its online pressroom also includes searchable press releases, plus bios and photos of current key executives as well as Nobel Prize winners and former CEOs. IBM is considering ways in which to push the envelope further with other features such as searchable transcripts of executives' press conferences, according to Matthew Anchin, manager of the Pressroom site. (For more on IBM's effort, see our interview with Anchin on page 80 in this chapter.)

Technology companies are not the only trailblazers in online newsrooms, however. Bethlehem Steel, which is a fraction of the size of Microsoft or IBM and is not exactly swimming in cash due to its Chapter 11 bankruptcy filing in October 2001, does an excellent job of making releases and images available online as well as executive bios and a history of the company. James D. Courtney, director of marketing communications, says the News Room dates back to 1996 and sprung from his need to bring order to the process of providing images to publications. Bethlehem has a rich archive of photos—including everything from executive portraits to images of bridges and other steel structures—that are requested regularly by magazine and newspaper editors around the world. (For more on how Courtney created the News Room and manages it cheaply, see our interview on page 82 in this chapter.)

Also deserving of praise is the Press Room of Air Products and Chemicals, Inc., which has covered all of its bases with searchable press releases, virtual press kits, company and business backgrounders and executive biographies, plus a detailed list of PR contacts, and a well-stocked Multimedia Gallery of photos and videos. Beth Mentesana, manager of corporate public relations, explains that the Web site helps the company serve not only reporters and editors, but also other constituents, such as business partners. She says the video gallery, for example, has enabled one of Air Products' technology providers to download "B-roll" footage of Air Products' manufacturing floor for use in its sales presentations. The gallery is much appreciated by its users, she says, and something that can be stocked without extraordinary effort if you think of it as a repository for materials created throughout the company, rather than as a showcase for only PR products. (For more on Air Products' press room, see our interview with Mentesana and her team on page 84 in this chapter.)

Smaller than even Bethlehem Steel or Air Products is Chemco, a Ferndale, Washington, maker of pressure-treated, fire-retardant exterior wood. Internet consultant Barry Bowen created a pressroom for the site at *chemco.org* that showcases recent releases, archives older releases, and prominently mentions the contact information for the company's PR person. In addition, recent press references are included in the pressroom along with video snippets that show how the flame retardant is applied to building materials.

"Any company doing PR, I think, can do a pressroom on a very modest budget," says Bowen, whose consultancy has its Web site at *bgroup.com*. He estimates startup costs of "a couple thousand bucks" for designing and establishing the pressroom. "The Web is just an additional dissemination tool or repository," he says. "The main thing is to get the basics done right. You don't need animation and a searchable database."

David Plenkovich, the manager of public relations for Chemco, says the pressroom is great for serving reporters who have heard about the company and drop by the site. He believes the site saves Chemco shipping costs that otherwise would be incurred to send out paper press kits, but he admits to worrying about the potential downside to having reporters serve themselves. "You may not have the opportunity to provide them with additional information or suggest new angles to the story," he says.

Like Bowen, other Web consultants and developers have carved out a place for themselves in the niche of the online pressroom. Among them is Wieck Media Services of Addison, Texas, which has done pressrooms for Honda and Toyota and manages online images for DaimlerChrysler, General Motors, and Ford. Wieck first went into business as an image distributor for *The New York Times* and then branched out into Internet development. Chairman and CEO James F. Wieck says working with his company is a wise investment whether it's managing the whole pressroom or just maintaining your database of images. "We save our clients tons of money," he says. "They used to send all that stuff out in hard press kits with three-ring binders full of slides."

Wieck says his clients decide how accessible they want their pressrooms or image archives to be. Some will require pressroom visitors to register to enter any part of the pressroom and others will require that step of only those people requesting high-resolution images. "They don't want people coming in and downloading an image and doing who knows what with it like putting it on a T-shirt and selling it," he says. Another reason to require registration, he says, is to track who has come to the pressroom and what releases those people have read. This intelligence can help the client a good deal, Wieck says, noting that the client can determine which releases are popular with which journalists and can determine that a reporter from a prominent publication needs to be contacted because he or she has failed to see an important press release.

Pressrooms do not need to be expensive, Wieck says, noting that templates can be used to simplify the design and management so that an investment of "a few thousand dollars" is sufficient to get the pressroom online. The next popular feature, he says, will be video clips a few seconds in length that can be downloaded for use by TV producers.

For every company like Chemco, Bethlehem Steel, or Microsoft, however, there are 10 companies that have not yet caught on to the importance of a well-functioning online pressroom. In our experience, it is clear that even the biggest, high-revenue companies still have a ways to go in making their pressrooms more useful.

Procter & Gamble, for example, had an easy-to-find link to "News" on its *pg.com* home page when we checked out the site in early 2002. The link took us to a Media Center that offered searchable press releases and other features, such as a Photo Gallery stocked with logos, product images, and executives' portraits. However, the company still offered executives' biographies in clunky PDF files, which produced server errors and unreadable files when we tried to access them. The list of PR contacts was also in a four-page PDF file, which is sure to enrage reporters on deadline who must nervously drum their fingers waiting for the file to download just to get a phone number for the appropriate PR person.

Other companies, like Prudential, had taken care of rudimentary things like a simple Web page of PR contacts and a list of press releases, but had failed to go the extra mile in making the press releases searchable or in providing photos or corporate backgrounders. Ford Motor Company had taken the trouble to sort its press releases under its various brands such as Lincoln and Jaguar, but it was impossible to find the name or telephone number for a PR representative. We also found the PR representatives at DaimlerChrysler with little reason to worry about being found on the Internet. Switchboard phone numbers for the headquarters in Germany and Michigan could be found by enterprising reporters who were willing to look beyond the "News" section of the company's site, which contains little more than press releases in reverse chronological order. DaimlerChrysler might deserve some credit for trying video reports in its newsroom, but how many busy journalists will take the time to watch daily TV reports produced for the company's employees?

B. L. Ochman, a marketing strategist and veteran public relations representative, frequently takes corporate pressrooms to task on her Web site, What's Next Online (*whatsnextonline.com*). Companies that fail to put contact information online are guilty of what she calls "the Wizard of Oz syndrome," in which they hide behind the curtain primarily because they're afraid of getting too many phone calls or e-mails from Web visitors. "The big companies think 'Oh my God, what if consumers can see what reporters see?'" she says with a laugh. "What a ridiculous concept." Companies that are locked into this mindset, she says, are failing to see the opportunity the Internet provides them to interact directly with consumers without the participation of reporters. "The media have always been the gatekeepers and they're not anymore," she says.

Ochman counsels companies to be helpful to journalists by putting as much information as possible online. "What are you hiding?" she asks. "There's nothing a reporter can't find on the Internet without you." She advises her clients to avoid creating barriers like registration forms for journalists and tells PR people not to worry about being cut out of the loop by displaying their information on the Web site. "I don't think there are very many journalists out there who are going to do their story from what they find on the Web site without calling anyone," she says.

The Internet is so important to public relations, Ochman argues, that PR people should not be content with just an online newsroom, and they should make sure management understands that not using the Internet as part of corporate PR is likely to cost more in the long run than the relatively minor cost of setting up and maintaining a Web site. "I don't think it's relevant whether it costs more or costs less," she says. "These are the tools we have to use." She suggests that PR people demonstrate to corporate executives how to use the Internet for research to impress on them how a Web site affects the image of the company. Prospective customers have their perceptions of a company shaped by the entire Web site—not just the pressroom—so public relations people should be in charge of the entire Web site, she says.

However, Ochman remains unconvinced that the PR industry will heed her advice and start using the Internet to its advantage. A big part of the problem, she says, is a continued preoccupation with getting ink from large media outlets like *The New York Times*. Clients, she says, need to be told that effective PR goes beyond a tally of clippings. She calls this RealityPR™. The Internet, she notes, is all about vertical marketing and it has presented PR people with a way to target their messages at the trade journals and the Web sites that cater to readers who do business in particular industries. The Internet should be used to build relationships with limited numbers of appropriate reporters and not as a means to broadcast product announcements to 1,000 journalists. "Journalists are not interested in your latest doodad," she says. "What they care about is how your doodad affects a lot of people and why."

What Ochman has observed about corporate pressrooms rings true with our own experiences and with what Internet usability guru Jakob Nielsen of the Nielsen Norman Group found in 2001 when he put the online pressrooms of major companies to the test. He found he was able to answer 60 percent of his questions online, which he describes as a decent success rate compared to the difficulties that Internet users often encounter in trying to complete other tasks, such as locating and purchasing merchandise. However, Nielsen notes that leaving 40 percent of questions unanswered is unacceptably high in the PR business and something that companies must work on if they are going to meet the needs of today's journalists. He echoes our frustration with corporate sites that fail to identify PR representatives, noting that 45 percent of the pressrooms he studied failed to include the telephone numbers of PR people who might come to the rescue of a journalist whose questions are not answered by the Web site.

Nielsen's report lists the top five reasons journalists use online pressrooms and the list rings true with our own experiences:

- Find a PR contact (name and telephone number)
- Check basic facts about the company (spelling of an executive's name, his or her age, headquarters location, etc.)
- Discover the company's own spin on events
- Check financial information
- Download images to use as illustrations in stories

The report also offered important advice for the types of files that companies should consider putting online. Although audio and video of press conferences featuring a company's CEO might be cutting edge, Nielsen notes that many journalists have slow Internet connections and are best served with simple HTML documents rather than PDFs or Flash presentations. Nielsen also points out the global reach of corporate Web sites and the resulting need, for example, to make date references clear. A press release should be dated October 3, 2002 for clarity's sake, he writes, because 10-03-02 will be read as March 10 by many overseas visitors and your site will be perceived as out of date.

IMPERATIVE #2: DON'T ELIMINATE HUMANS

Although it is imperative to empower journalists to find information on their own, we think it's important that PR representatives not lose sight of the need to have people available on the phone or in person to answer reporters' queries. In Deirdre Breakenridge's own experience as PR representative for JVC Professional Products Company, she found that having a well-stocked newsroom did not necessarily decrease the need for human contact. The site for the electronics manufacturer had technical product specifications, suggested retail prices, high-resolution images of products, logos, product comparisons, case studies of users, and other features. However, JVC noticed that editors need to be assisted through the online information-gathering process. Most editors find the contact information for the PR agency and then call to verify they have the right information. In other cases, some editors say they are just too busy to go through the online newsroom and prefer to make a quick call to the PR contact to request that copies of the appropriate documents be sent to them.

THE FLIP SIDE

We talk more in future chapters about how the Internet's impact on journalism is changing the role of PR people. It's worth pointing out here, though, that the other significant impact that the Internet has had on public relations is a rise in the number of news-oriented sites with constant demands for copy. It is true that more than a few went bust in the recession, but many others have survived with shrunken editorial staffs more desperate than ever for copy. In some cases, reporters have been taken almost entirely out of the equation and there are opportunities for PR people to have their press releases published without much editorial review.

As we mentioned earlier in our two scenarios involving *The Smalltown Gazette*, sites like Yahoo! Finance give immediate play to any press release you distribute over Business Wire or

PR Newswire, ensuring that the release is featured with all other news about your public company. However, there are many more sites, ranging from management consultants to health maintenance organizations (HMOs) that are so hungry for editorial content that they will pick up releases from the major distributors. "The Net has changed what we all think of as the media resources we need to work with," says Sharon VanSickle, general manager of Fleishman-Hillard's Pacific Northwest offices. She notes that press releases FH develops for its clients are often posted on sites operated by financial institutions or consultants, and on news-oriented Web sites created to serve niche markets, such as the use of technology in the trucking or health-care industries. This means that care should be taken to write the releases in an accessible language that is appropriate for consumers.

Our own experience tells us that even traditional news organizations are more willing to publish press releases verbatim or in edited form in their online venues than they would ordinarily do in print. A major reason for this is that many publications have squeezed existing staff for the additional copy needed to feed the publication's Web site, so reporters are often frantic to find something they can contribute every day or sometimes twice a day to fulfill their online obligations. These Internet-driven demands amount to an open door for PR people who are familiar with a publication and its online cousin and are able to offer up suitable releases that lend themselves to quick reports. A release that includes the who, what, where, when, and why of an event, plus some context from an industry analyst, stands a good chance of getting published on a lot of Web sites without much editorial interference.

Of course, it's good to remember B. L. Ochman's rule about looking beyond press releases concerning your "latest doodad." She counsels her clients to develop Top 10 lists and helpful articles that are not sales oriented that can help satisfy Web site editors' demands for copy and help to build a perception of your client as a trusted expert.

In our next chapter, we focus on the ways in which e-mail can be used more effectively to get your client's message out to the right journalists and opinion makers.

IBM has had an online Pressroom since early 1996 and Matthew Anchin, manager of its operations, has been responsible for the site since mid-1999. The mission of the Pressroom, he says, is to help journalists in their coverage of IBM. It is not considered a money-saver because the site is "synergistic with day-to-day PR, not a replacement."

A link labeled "Journalists" on the IBM home page (*ibm.com*) brings Net users to the Pressroom. However, Anchin knows that the service attracts more than working press. "What the Internet has done is make everything available to everyone," he says. "It brings the public back into 'public relations.'" Of course, IBM could have taken a different approach and required prospective users of its Pressroom to complete a registration form to get a password for the site, but Anchin says that would have been a bad idea. "My audience won't put up with that. They won't stand for it," he says. "That tends to be a significant barrier to entry."

Key features of the Pressroom include a searchable archive of press releases that is updated in a timely fashion when new releases are sent out through wire services. The releases can be browsed chronologically and are sorted into categories to provide what Anchin calls "multiple views of the information." Background data about the company is updated quarterly to reflect the latest employee headcount, business locations, and other facts. A database of PR practitioners is maintained on the site so that reporters can identify and contact the person responsible for a particular technology or unit of the company. Anchin says the idea of using a single *PR@ibm.com* e-mail box was never considered. "We're here to work with journalists, so why should we be erecting barriers?" he asks. The price to pay for publicizing the personal e-mail addresses of PR reps is a few misdirected e-mails from consumers who need help with a product or ask about a warranty. "We try our best to handle them," he says, explaining that those e-mails can be forwarded very easily to the appropriate departments.

To guarantee that press releases can be posted quickly, staff members in the corporate communications department have the ability to add new releases to the Web site automatically without the assistance of a Webmaster or other technical personnel.

Anchin says IBM has high standards for its Web sites—and it must—because the public expects a lot from a technology company. Nevertheless, Big Blue faces the same challenges that Web site operators are grappling with in just about any industry. Chief among them is the need to unify the Web efforts of various internal groups, while updating services that were built on technologies that are no longer on the cutting edge. "You're trying to solve some of the problems you created for yourself when the Web was this new thing," Anchin says.

Of particular concern for IBM is the fact that it does business in 160 countries, which means that a variety of PR practitioners are operating different IBM Pressroom sites around the world. An obvious goal is to integrate their operations so they are not all struggling to keep their sites current. "We're embarking on the next evolutionary step on how this site works and how it works with other country sites out there," Anchin says, explaining that one goal is to build a common back-end system that could feed releases onto the various IBM sites. A more powerful search engine is also on the wish list, he says.

Anchin acknowledges all the predictions about faster Internet connection speeds, but he isn't running to load up IBM's Pressroom with streaming media files. IBM's Investor Relations department offers Webcasts of financial press conferences, he notes, but the Pressroom is not planning to stock up on audio and video right now. "I'm not fully convinced that's what journalists are looking for yet," he says. "I'm not sure journalists want to sit and listen to a whole speech," he adds. "Maybe transcripts would be better."

IBM gets unsolicited feedback from journalists and occasionally asks questions of Pressroom visitors to determine what other features or improvements are needed. Anchin acknowledges that it also helps to keep an eye on what other companies are doing in their online newsrooms. He says the majority of IBM Pressroom's visitors are doing basic research that involves searches of press releases and following links to other *ibm.com* pages that offer greater detail about the company's products.

Anchin suggests that the Pressroom's biggest impact on the day-to-day activities of IBM's PR people might be that fewer images are mailed out on Zip disks because image files are now online for quick downloads. However, making information available for the taking has not greatly reduced the number of phone calls IBM receives. "The press site has helped journalists find out fast who they need to talk to," Anchin says. Reporters still seek out PR people who are knowledgeable about a subject area and can help to put the latest news into context and line up interview subjects. "The value PR plays to a company has not gone away," he says, noting that the future might see more PR people with engineering degrees who are able to educate reporters about IBM's technology and vision.

Finally, we asked Anchin if IBM had calculated the return on investment of its Pressroom. His answer implied that such figures would be confidential, but he added: "We are investing in a new, bigger, better Pressroom. I would say that is pretty good testament to what we think of it." ■

PR INTERVIEW:
BETHLEHEM STEEL'S JAMES D. COURTNEY

James D. Courtney makes it plain to an interviewer that he's no techie. He also doesn't consider himself an Internet visionary. As Bethelehem Steel's director of marketing communications, he pushed the company to establish a Web site in 1996 because he thought it was good for branding, but he also saw it as a solution for old paper-based systems that were just too difficult to keep up with.

In particular, Courtney says he and the company's small PR staff were tired of fielding last-minute requests from frenzied magazine or newspaper editors who needed a photo of the Golden Gate Bridge, the Delaware Memorial Bridge, or any other steel structure in Bethlehem's large photo archive. Each request required someone to go through files and get the photo into the mail and then refile images that were returned.

Digital photography was not a hot topic in 1996, but Courtney saw the Internet's applicability and hired an outside service to scan the most requested images and put them on *bethsteel.com* in a feature called Image Bank. The News Room and Image Bank soon grew "like topsy," Courtney says, and he began doing his own scanning and posting of images. Press releases are added to the News Room by simply converting Microsoft Word files to HTML and posting them. A PDF version is also offered for each release in case reporters want to print them out. The releases can be searched by the Web site's overall search function, which returns hits on all active files on the Web server regardless of whether they are in the News Room or in other areas of the site.

Courtney says his philosophy has been to make all information conveniently accessible to journalists without the need for passwords or registration. "How important is it to keep satisfied the people who have your reputation in their hands when they put pen to paper?" he asks.

The one exception to his open-access rule is in Bethlehem's handling of high-resolution images. Low-resolution images are available on the site, but Courtney requires anyone seeking a high-resolution image to fill out an online form that indicates where the image is to be printed. The requests are forwarded to Courtney, who then puts the image on the Web server and e-mails a specific URL to the requester where he or she can retrieve the image. Keeping all the high-resolution images off the Web server saves the server from the burden of an extra gigabyte of data, he says, but more important, the request process gives Bethlehem an opportunity to monitor who is using its images. Reporters and photo editors have the minor inconvenience of filling out the form, he argues, but they still get the requested images more quickly than in pre-Internet days and Bethlehem gets the benefit of knowing how images are used. The company has determined that about 80 percent of the requests for high-resolution images are from the news media, 10 percent are from engineers and academics interested in steelmaking, and 10 percent are from schoolchildren working on term papers. The company has also weeded out suspicious requests for images of bridges and other structures from Web visitors who failed to state a reason for their requests in the days of heightened security awareness following the September 11, 2001 terrorist attacks.

Courtney says his experience tells him that a strong online pressroom is even more important for a small company than a large one. "You better do this if you don't have a PR staff of 25," he says. "Get it digitized and get it available for self-serve."

Bethlehem's News Room was designed as part of its overall Web site, which Courtney says was done for "about $50K." He says Bethlehem is now able to update 99 percent of the site's content on its own without a developer's assistance, which means that maintaining the site is not expensive. ■

Beth Mentesana, a 24-year PR veteran, has not been manager of corporate PR at Air Products for very long, so she still views the company sort of like an outsider and remains impressed with its commitment to the Internet as an important component of the overall communications process. The company has an internal graphic design/Web development team and that has certainly helped the PR department in its efforts to keep its online Press Room updated with the latest releases and other pertinent information. "They're willing to commit money and resources to doing this well and keeping it fresh not only because it's the smart thing to do, but also because our measurement studies and focus groups confirm its value to our businesses," she says.

Joe Eilenberg, supervisor of the company's graphic design team, says the PR group also has leveraged its resources well by collecting materials from various parts of the nearly $6-billion company, which has 14 different strategic units. Instead of filling the Press Room with materials created only for PR purposes, the PR group has viewed the Web pages as an online repository for resources created throughout the company. This means that some of the photos or videos in the Multimedia Gallery might have been created to support a marketing campaign, investors' conference, or an employee meeting. Images from the annual report are in the database, as are some videos created for internal training.

"I think the whole video portion is a developing area," says Mentesana. She recalls one instance in which the availability of video clips online helped a technology supplier that wanted to include footage of an Air Products factory floor in a sales presentation that boasted of the supplier's top customers. The supplier was able to get the video quickly without having to ask Air Products to put a videotape in the mail.

"Webcasting is also increasing in demand," Mentesana points out, "as shareholders, employees, and the media want real-time information, as well as the option to see and hear replays of Webcasted financial conferences and press conferences." Mentesana notes that Air Products is now Webcasting all of its quarterly financial teleconferences and will do the same for major press announcements.

Katie Zamolyi, a former senior communications specialist on the company's e-business team, says the three-year-old online Press Room saves time that used to be spent on tracking down and mailing out logos, backgrounders, photos, and other information. Mentasana adds that the time saved is now used more effectively. "Having this capability gives us more time to spend on coming up with story ideas, making phone calls, and meeting with editors," she says. "Regardless of how sophisticated we are technologically, we are still dealing with people. True relationships are built through phone conversations and face-to-face interactions."

Mentesana says she has never worried that a well-stocked Press Room might cause reporters not to call her PR team. "It's incumbent upon us to engage," she says. "We have to take the time to find out who covers us and where we want our audience to read about us." Zamolyi, meanwhile, notes that while the Press Room helps reporters understand the complex company's structure and products, they still have questions. "We still get a lot of calls," she reports.

The Press Room also figures prominently in Air Products' plans for emergencies, says Mentasana, who notes that "dark" Web pages have been developed that could be switched on immediately in the unlikely event of a crisis. "If we don't fill the vacuum of information, somebody else will," she says.

Eilenberg says one important lesson Air Products has learned from its Web experience is to keep only one copy of a press release or other resource on its site to facilitate easy updating. Business units that might want to showcase the release should place a pointer on their Web pages rather than a copy of the document, he says, so that the PR staff can make corrections or updates on only that one document. This principle is something the PR department is keeping in mind as it seeks to work more closely with the company's Web sites in various countries, says Debbie Bauer, communications coordinator for the PR group. One goal is to make sure that the people responsible for Web pages in other countries all point back to the original document in the main Press Room, she notes. "Without that, you risk having inconsistent information in different areas of the company's Web site," she says.

Having an up-to-date, easy-to-navigate online Press Room has made my job more efficient," Bauer adds, "because I can respond immediately to editors' needs. Rather than produce something and put it in the mail, I can direct them to the Press Room where the information and visuals they need are readily available. In some cases, that may make the difference between being able to meet a tight deadline resulting in positive coverage versus getting no mention at all."

Mentesana inserts a final note: "Having someone like Debbie, who takes her role as a Press Room coordinator very seriously, is our 'secret weapon.' You need an organized, detail-oriented individual in this role, who knows the company, has good interpersonal skills, understands the PR profession, and maintains a sense of urgency about keeping information consistent and current. ∎

JOURNALIST INTERVIEW: PROFESSOR DIANNE LYNCH OF ST. MICHAEL'S COLLEGE

Dianne Lynch is certain that she could not have the career she has right now if it weren't for the Internet.

For one thing, it has provided her with fodder for her scholarly pursuits as an associate professor of journalism at St. Michael's College in Vermont. She has written a book called *Virtual Ethics: Debating Media Values in a Digital Age* (Coursewise, 1998) about the difficulties in distinguishing between editorial and advertising content. She is also doing research for the Online News Association, which represents Internet news sites. However, Lynch is also a working journalist and addicted to the Internet as an information source for what she writes. "I could not have lived in Vermont and done the kind of journalism I do now 10 years ago," she says.

Originally a newspaperwoman from Wisconsin, Lynch has contributed to *USA Today* and *The Christian Science Monitor*, and most recently has written a regular column about women and technology for ABCNEWS's *abcnews.com*. What she has seen in a 20-year career, she says, is a remarkable shifting of relationships between journalists and PR people. "They were the people who decided when and where and how you got the information that you needed to do your job," she says of PR professionals. "There was a symbiosis there."

The Internet, Lynch argues, has made journalists more autonomous because they are now able to get press kits online and locate phone numbers or e-mail addresses for top executives without the help of PR people. "There's no longer a need from the journalist's perspective to go to that gatekeeper," she says. "We want to be the decision makers."

"I can't remember the last time I talked to a PR agency," says Lynch, who explains how successful she's been in using the Internet to get the home and office phone numbers of top corporate brass. Details about companies and their products are in their online pressrooms or available through third parties like Hoover's Online or the SEC's Edgar database. Other services like Google make it possible to find out what customers have said about a company or its products in any of thousands of online newsgroups or discussion boards. "There are just too many places for journalists to get information," says Lynch.

PR people can still make themselves relevant to journalists by providing them with special insights or a timely heads-up before an announcement, Lynch says, but most have not. The typical PR e-mail appears to be part of a mass mailing sent out to blanket a huge media list rather than a personalized message to a select group of journalists with whom the PR person is trying to build a relationship, Lynch notes. "And relationships are more key than ever because we don't *have* to go to them."

This failure to use e-mail to strengthen relationships is one example of how PR people have not recognized the extent to which the Internet has changed their relationship with journalists, Lynch says. "I don't know that I think PR is going to go away, but I think its role is definitely going to change," she says. She suggests that PR people will come to recognize that they cannot stand between their clients and the press and will, instead, see their role as helping their clients deliver their message more effectively. PR people might need to become better versed in business strategies, psychology, marketing, and even public speaking, Lynch says. A good place to start might be to focus on making the top executives who are now more exposed to the press into better representatives of their companies, she notes. "Many of them don't understand the concept of a core message."

In addition, Lynch recommends that PR people become more expert at learning about what's on the Internet. She recalls the example of former Infoseek executive Patrick Naughton, who was arrested on sex charges in

1999 based on his conversations in a chat room with an undercover police officer. "There's no such thing as being invisible online anymore," she notes. "PR people need to know where their clients are leaving tracks."

As for the Internet's impact on journalism beyond day-to-day information gathering, Lynch sees her location in Vermont as indicative of a larger trend. "The power centers around journalism are shifting," she says, noting that it is no longer important to be in New York City or Washington, DC, if the same information is available online from Wisconsin or Montana. This means that readers benefit from getting a "diversity of perspectives," she adds. "I'm an Internet zealot if there ever was one," she confesses. "I really believe it has shifted fundamentally the sources of information and the nature of that information." ∎

7 Using E-Mail Smartly

> Just because it's cheap, don't abuse it.

> Don't hit "send" too quickly.

> "It's only an e-mail" cannot be an excuse for sloppiness.

As important as a top-notch online pressroom is to your overall PR strategy, we all know that the reporters at the publications you seek to target are probably not going to just flock to your online newsroom. E-mail is most likely the tool that you'll use to attract their attention and get them interested in your client. In this chapter, we discuss how to use the tool effectively, how to avoid some of the errors made in the early days of e-mail, and the need to be vigilant in upholding your standards even when using a medium as informal as e-mail.

Strangely enough, you could actually argue that e-mail and public relations are not a good match for one another. Consider this list of the ways in which e-mail contradicts many of the practices that PR professionals consider to be sound:

■ E-mail has the ability to reach the masses. PR, on the contrary, is extremely targeted.

■ The premise behind e-mail is quick communication. PR teaches executives to formulate messages carefully.

- E-mail is a relaxed form of communication that often neglects punctuation, proper spelling, and grammar, and is not formal by nature. Do we even have to comment on what professionals are taught regarding all forms of communication, spoken and written?
- Because e-mail correspondence is relaxed, there's a tendency to type quickly and worry about what was said after the writer clicks Send. This type of practice is unheard of in PR textbooks.
- E-mail is rarely proofread the way PR professionals are taught to proofread. Honestly, how many people read their e-mail backwards to catch spelling errors?

Now, with so many sticking points, why are PR professionals stuck on e-mail? There are numerous reasons (speed and ease of use come to mind immediately). We've put together some basic principles that we think will help you use e-mail effectively without falling into some of the traps we've just mentioned.

HOW TO USE E-MAIL EFFECTIVELY

PRINCIPLE #1: EASE OF DISTRIBUTION DOES NOT NECESSARILY MEAN DISTRIBUTION TO THE MASSES

This is probably the biggest misunderstanding that PR people, as a whole, have had about e-mail. Given the fact that e-mail is practically free, many people have decided that e-mailing 200 journalists is better than e-mailing only 50. This thinking seemed to be particularly common during the dot-com craze when startups desperate for the attention they needed to attract customers, employees, and additional funding, were especially guilty of e-mailing long lists of media contacts. Some of them even committed the cardinal sin of leaving the names of e-mail recipients exposed at the top of the message so the confidentiality of those addresses was compromised to everyone else on the list. Large-scale "e-mail blasts" to long lists of reporters produced many cries of "Spam!" and helped to lower the esteem of PR people in the eyes of many reporters. Their complaints were communicated to clients, who generally don't like being called spammers, and now it is more common for clients to ask questions about how many reporters will be receiving their e-mailed press releases and how those recipients are to be selected.

Consider the following example of a client who was so concerned about the stigma of being labeled a spammer that he had lots of questions for his PR agency about the numbers of e-mail messages it was sending out on behalf of his architectural firm. The PR agency had provided him with more than 10 e-mail lists, with at least 50 media outlets per list. The media lists included educational, municipal, architectural, engineering, real estate, and regional and national newspapers, to name a few. The CEO of this architectural firm had every right to be concerned with this large list and so he quickly called his PR account executive. The CEO explained his concerns regarding spamming to the PR executive, who immediately recognized that the PR firm had not adequately explained its e-mail practices. The PR person then explained that not every release would go to all of the different media outlets on the various master lists that the client had in his possession. Criteria such as the type of architectural project developed by the firm and the type of news involving the firm, the readership demographics of a particular publication, and the type of news covered by the media outlet, would be used in determining who got which releases. The PR account executive reinforced to the CEO that although the process had changed to Internet distribution, it was still extremely targeted using the appropriate lists, which were always verified for accuracy. The agency continued to employ its policy of only distributing to media people who wanted to receive the architectural firm's correspondence. In addition, the agency abided by the requests of any editors who asked for their correspondence in another fashion. Lastly, if an editor wanted to be removed from the e-mail distribution list, his or her request was granted.

The CEO required no further explanation and his fears of being known as a spammer subsided. Although this scenario had a happy ending, it illustrates how sensitive many clients have become and how important it is for PR people to do the legwork that needs to be done to compile targeted media lists with e-mail addresses of appropriate journalists.

PRINCIPLE #2: QUICK COMMUNICATION VIA E-MAIL DOES NOT MEAN POORLY FORMULATED MESSAGES

Just because you can type up an e-mail and send it out quickly that doesn't mean you have to do things that way. In fact, the quickness of e-mail gives us time we can use to make press releases better than they might have been in the past. More people in more locations can be involved in drafting and approving the releases before they are e-mailed to reporters.

Our point is illustrated by the example of a manager of marketing communications at a well-known electronics manufacturer who needed to get a news release out in response to a competitor's announcement. E-mails started to circulate among several executives of the electronics firm and the PR agency. The normal news release process between this agency and its client usually involved just one PR account executive and the marketing communications manager, who would pass a draft or two back and forth. However, this announcement was different and involved at least three executives forwarding revisions and information to the agency for further development of the release. During the process other members of the electronics firm (not involved with the revisions) circulated messages such as the following, "Let's act swiftly!" and "We have to get our message out quickly." Despite the pressure to move forward prematurely, the release rolled out successfully when all the parties were satisfied with the company's message. Due to the nature and sensitivity of the communication, the act of using e-mail internally to formulate the proper message, and not rush out with a half-baked message, was a strategic decision that enhanced the firm's position in the eyes of the media and customers.

Despite a natural tendency to use e-mail for quick communication, the preceding example illustrates how a company was able to take the proper amount of time to construct a news release that strategically addressed a critical issue. The use of e-mail back and forth between many executives and the PR agency facilitated communication and produced a stronger message that was distributed to the media. In the pre–e-mail age, it would have taken twice as long to get this message correct.

We recognize that our example might be an exception to the regular practice given the tremendous attraction of striking quickly with an e-mailed release regardless of its quality. It's easy to imagine a PR professional shortening the drafting process by arguing that "too many hands are in the pot" or a client so eager to get a message out that he or she might rush the formulating process. We urge PR professionals to resist the pressures to short-circuit the message formulation process. Instead of thinking of e-mail as a tool that pushes us to act quickly, we should see it as something that awards us the extra time that we need to make our message better and more effective.

PRINCIPLE #3: THERE'S NO EXCUSE FOR CARELESS CORRESPONDENCE

E-mail is not, by any means, an excuse to communicate with errors, such as mistakes in grammar, punctuation, and spelling. The PR professional is trained to communicate in an effort to create a positive impression, image, or perception. In PR, we communicate to impress, and with every communication a company has its brand image to uphold. You've heard the popular saying, "First impressions are lasting." Well, on the Internet, with every impression (not just the first), you must live up to a customer's standards. Proper communication is always expected. Any imperfections in communication are a direct reflection on a brand. Not only does the brand suffer from sloppy communication, so does the PR person who is sending the message (in the case of e-mail). Remember, even if your client forwards a sloppy message to you that does not have punctuation or contains spelling mistakes, you know better. PR professionals and the brands they support are judged via any communication channel, so don't let your guard down. You're always being judged.

One client gave its PR firm a terrible tongue lashing over a spelling error in an e-mail that was circulated internally between the PR agency and the company's marketing team. The marketing director was candid with the PR person when she stated, "Quite frankly, it makes me a little nervous about what your agency sends out on our behalf." Even though the PR person's first reaction might be, "It's only an e-mail," there's still no excuse. Professionals and their companies are judged by the way they present themselves in correspondence, and e-mail is no different. There's definitely a time and a place for relaxed correspondence. For instance, typing e-mail to a friend or business colleague of equal rank, in shortened sentences and without careful attention to grammar, is a common practice. However, there are situations in which you should think twice about using relaxed e-mails forwarded between the following parties:

- Client and PR agency (watch the punctuation and the grammar, no matter how long you have worked with a company)
- Company and its stakeholders (this includes communication with employees, suppliers, distributors, shareholders, etc.)
- Employees and their supervisors or senior management in the company
- PR professionals and the media
- Company executives and the media

Another attribute of e-mail that is worth remembering here is that it is easily forwarded. The relaxed or carelessly written e-mail you might intend to share with only senior managers could end up in a reporter's inbox if any of those managers wishes to share it. Such was the case in March 2000 at Cerner Corporation, a health-care software development company, when an e-mail memo intended for Cerner's managers became the subject of coverage in *The New York Times*. The CEO clicked Send too quickly without fully evaluating the possible repercussions of such an e-mail. For a company that was known for its friendly reputation, the e-mail memo was less than friendly. It contained angry tones and divulged a host of sensitive issues surely not meant to be publicized. What was in that memo that was so damaging? Instead of coming across as a motivating message from the CEO, which it was originally intended to be, the e-mail was condescending, scolding, and somewhat threatening to its recipients. In the e-mail, the CEO of Cerner Corporation chewed out the intended recipients using the following verbiage: "As managers you do not know what your employees are doing; or do not care . . . . In either case, you have a problem and you will fix it or I will replace you." A strong closing phrase was really the straw that broke the camel's back: "You have 2 weeks. Tick tock." For Cerner Corporation, this e-mail affected the company's good reputation with a stock price that plummeted from $44 to approximately $30 in the same month. An amalgamation of the damaging communication, the lack of respect paid to Cerner's own employees on the receiving end of the intended communication, and the marred image was enough to make this company quickly realize the magnitude of the error. It didn't matter how friendly Cerner appeared to be on its Web site or what other type of communication it presented to its stakeholders; its reputation suffered.

PRINCIPLE #4: AS TEDIOUS AS IT SOUNDS, E-MAIL COMMUNICATION DESERVES PROOFREADING WITH THE SAME SCRUTINY AS A SNAIL MAIL LETTER IN CERTAIN CIRCUMSTANCES

Would you be telling a small white lie to yourself, your boss, or your client if you said you proofread 100 percent of your outgoing e-mails with precision? We recommend making a conscious effort to determine which e-mails deserve the most careful attention. One PR firm that we interviewed admitted that even the CEO of the company was forwarding e-mails both internally to his employees as well as to new and existing clients without checking his work. Another senior-level executive of an integrated communications firm noted how dangerous it is to have e-mail addresses pop-up automatically as you type them. This executive learned a harsh lesson when he inadvertently forwarded confidential information to an employee of the firm who had a name similar to that of the intended executive recipient. For example, the e-mail meant for jmartin@xyzcompany.com might end up with jmarino@xyz-company.com if you are not careful.

Because communication travels at the speed of light and negative news seems to spread even more quickly, it is imperative to check and recheck e-mail correspondence. There are several ways to screen your e-mail for potential problems:

- Professionals should not rely on only spelling and grammar checks—errors can still slip through the cracks.
- As a precaution, some PR professionals type e-mail correspondence into a word processing document, proofread with at least two sets of eyes, and then cut and paste it into the body of the e-mail.
- Professionals are also learning to proofread subject lines and pay particular attention to keying in e-mail addresses correctly.
- Sending test e-mails to yourself and colleagues is becoming an increasingly common practice as professionals realize that what they put into the body of a text e-mail or an HTML e-mail is not necessarily what the recipient sees.

PRINCIPLE #5: KNOW THE PREFERENCE OF YOUR RECIPIENTS

Just as you wouldn't want someone filling your fax machine with pages and pages of unwanted information, many e-mail recipients are very protective of their inboxes and do not appreciate large e-mail messages that are slow to download or attachments that could be a means for delivering viruses. Although many of us in PR and journalism have accepted the virus threat as a cost of doing business more easily with attached documents, many others remain steadfastly opposed to opening all attachments and are resentful of anyone who tries to sneak one into their inboxes. For this reason, we advise you to use simple text messages to solicit interest in your clients and to then inquire as to whether it is appropriate to send along backgrounders and other press kit materials that might be in PDFs or text documents. By all means, definitely ask before sending along Microsoft PowerPoint presentations as attachments. Even the most patient and forgiving among us are bound to get angry while waiting for a huge PowerPoint attachment to squeeze its way through our skinny dial-up connection.

PRINCIPLE #6: SEND IT ONLY ONCE AND MOVE ON

Countless reporters have complained to us about PR professionals who hound them about whether they've received an e-mail. The technology is now reliable enough that it is generally safe to assume that your message has been received successfully. One good way to double-check this is to send your press releases to yourself at several different e-mail addresses. A free Hotmail or Yahoo! account can show you that the e-mail left your company and crossed the Internet to other mail servers. Another step worth taking is cross-checking your e-mail list against the lists you use to fax and snail mail the same release. Scott Jaschik, editor of *The Chronicle of Higher Education*, is among many editors we know who are peeved about seeing the same release in his e-mail, in a fax, and then in his mailbox two days later. He notes that the releases he deletes from his e-mail do not magically become more interesting to him when he gets the fax or snail mail copy. "Somewhere out there in PR land, there's a myth that the more ways you send it the better," he says. (For more on Jaschik's observations about e-mail, see our interview with him on page 104 in this chapter.)

E-MAIL CAMPAIGNS

As we've noted throughout this book, the Internet has provided us all with a means of reaching not only our traditional constituency of reporters, but also the general public that is now accessible to us, often without the interference of journalists. In the same way that e-mail helps us to reach out quickly to reporters, it also enables us to communicate with the very people who are going to spend money with our clients. For this reason, coordinated e-mail campaigns are becoming more popular and are meeting with success when they are designed, implemented, and tracked properly.

Heidi Anderson is a Colorado-based freelance writer who has written about e-mail campaigns for marketing Web site ClickZ. Her experience has taught her that the best campaigns generally relate to smaller "impulse buys" that people are willing to make when they receive an e-mail. The National Dine Out America campaign conducted by Red Lobster's parent company Darden Restaurants is a good example of this, Anderson notes, because the e-mail encouraged recipients to come to Red Lobster on a particular night in October 2001 when all the profits would be donated to the victims of the September 11 terrorist attacks. (For more on Darden's campaign, see our interview with Rick Walsh, senior vice president of corporate affairs, on page 99 in this chapter.) In contrast, an e-mail campaign related to a large purchase, such as a new car, is going to be much harder to track in terms of effectiveness. Some recipients might click on the e-mail to learn more about the car on the Web, but their ultimate buying decision is likely to be weeks or months removed and will probably be influenced by print and TV ads, comparative research, and a test drive.

Anderson's belief that e-mail campaigns can work best for impulse buys is supported by the success of The Venetian, a five-star Las Vegas hotel that turned to e-mail to fill up empty rooms following the September 11 attacks. Its e-mail heralded technologies sure to be more widely used in the future of e-mail marketing, including both video from TV commercials and a "call now" button that enabled recipients to telephone the hotel immediately to take advantage of the discount rates trumpeted in the e-mail.

Undertaking an e-mail campaign aimed at thousands of consumers is not a small task. We strongly recommend contracting with a professional e-mail distributor to send out your messages. These companies, which include DoubleClick and CheetahMail, have huge farms of mail servers capable of sending out thousands of e-mails in a short amount of time. They usually charge several hundred dollars to set up an account and your mailing lists and then a cost-per-thousand rate (CPM) that can be anywhere from $8 to $15 with lower rates for large volumes. These companies are also adept at handling the bounce-backs that occur due to server errors or bad addresses and they will even intercede on your behalf with spam police such as the Mail Abuse Prevention System (MAPS), who might try to block your mail if you are accused of spamming. Of course, we strongly urge you to greatly reduce your chances of being accused of spamming by directing your e-mail campaign only at recipients who have agreed to receive your e-mail. We discuss this topic in greater depth in our next chapter, which is devoted to opt-in, permission based e-mail.

PR INTERVIEW:
RICK WALSH OF DARDEN RESTAURANTS

"At Darden Restaurants, we always think in terms of the team,* and it was a particularly talented team of people that made the National Dine Out For America e-mail campaign such a huge success," states Walsh. The result was a communication strategy that raised over $1.5 million for the 9/11 Disaster Relief Fund of the American Red Cross. We asked Walsh about the specifics of the National Dine Out For America campaign and why he felt it was successful. Here's how Walsh responded to our interview questions:

Q: Does Darden prefer e-mail campaigns to traditional advertising campaigns?

A: Both have their strengths. We use consumer research in everything we do from restaurant planning to communication strategies and we stay close to our customers by using a variety of different communication tools. An e-mail campaign gives us the overall flexibility we need as well as the means to target different tastes and interests. It is cost effective and we receive a great deal of valuable e-mail feedback as well. Although the telephone, mail, and customer cards are used to evaluate our restaurants, we feel that e-mail feedback is growing quickly as a very important way to stay in touch with our customers.

Q: Why did you select an e-mail campaign for the National Dine Out For America campaign?

A: We felt that because of the circumstances and the horrific events of September 11, an e-mail campaign was the most unobtrusive and respectful method for our customers. There was a great deal of emotional uncertainty after 9/11 and we wanted to show people there was a way for them to help by dining out and that there was no monetary gain for Darden. The campaign reinforced Darden's values and left it up to the customers to make the choice of whether or not they would dine out to raise money. This strategy also gave all of us, employees and customers alike, a way to do something to help.

Q: What were some of the other options you considered and why did you rule them out?

A: Darden uses network advertising very effectively. Historically we would have used this type of advertising. However, time was a factor and we had less than 30 days to put all this together. From the time the employees of a restaurant company in Seattle came up with the idea, to the time we decided to participate, there was only so much communication that could be coordinated. We decided e-mail would be the most effective strategy and adding a viral component (send to a friend) enhanced the campaign response. The e-mail blast factor gave us the leg up we needed and was coordinated with an in-restaurant promotion inviting our customers, vendors, friends, and family to participate.

Q: Discuss the design of the e-mail and its subject line.

A: The design had to be simple and the message straightforward in order to be effective. We included the logo and information as well as a restaurant locator link so recipients could find the closest Darden restaurant near his or her home. The subject line was probably the most important line of the e-mail. It's the line that catches the recipient's attention. We used "For Those Who Hunger to Help" as our lead. The e-mail's design and message appealed to people who were looking for a way to help out in the tragedy and who wanted to make a difference and participate in National Dine Out For America.

Q: How many people responded to the e-mail?

A: Tracking can be an unbelievably difficult exercise. It was difficult to truly know how many recipients actually responded, but we do know the following. Several hundred thousand people participated in National Dine Out For America. Over 73,000 people opened the e-mail and received more content and details. Approximately 25,000 people accessed the restaurant locator to check for a restaurant closest to them.

Q: Were there any respondents who said they could not read the HTML e-mail?

A: We had user-specified viewing preferences so regardless of format, our customers were able to view it.

Q: Do you feel you were successful in your campaign efforts?

A: Absolutely. Dine Out For America was on a Thursday night (not a particularly busy night) and the restaurants were much more crowded than usual. Many were swamped! We raised over $1.5 million, more than half a million more than we expected. We feel we were able to communicate an important message to people, give them a way to help without being in New York, Washington, or Pennsylvania, and the restaurant teams really delivered a special experience for our customers. I think it helped all of us feel like we were really doing something to help and we may have even attracted some new customers in the process.

Q: Are you planning any future e-mail campaigns?

A: Yes, we are, but in very different ways. We will generate new campaigns to promote benefits for our customers and national promotions. However, we will not use the viral strategy unless it's a unique circumstance, as in the case of 9/11. We are very respectful of e-mail and expect to use it very judiciously. In general our two core business, Red Lobster and Olive Garden, use focused e-mail a bit more frequently. Red Lobster currently uses e-mail once a month for national promotions and Olive Garden distributes three monthly electronic newsletters (focusing on restaurant news and events, wine, and recipes).

Q: Are there any issues or challenges when using e-mail that you would like to discuss?

A: When you use e-mail keep it simple. You should avoid burdening customers with too many communications (no spamming). We try to make all of our communication valuable and actionable. We also try to have some kind of measurement of the response (when we use e-mail campaigns we notice that the traffic on our Web site increases). Lastly, you must provide your e-mail recipients with a means to talk back and give their suggestions, grievances, etc. Darden has an entire department dedicated to receiving and responding to feedback from our guests.

Q: What are some trends with e-mail that you have noticed?

A: There are several trends upon which you may want to focus when planning an Internet or e-mail communications strategy:

- **Search engine focus:** It is critical your Web site be search engine friendly.

- **Performance focus:** Make sure that what your doing is reputable and complimentary to your brand.

- **Quality not quantity focus:** The quality of the communication is what enhances customer loyalty, not the quantity. Make it good and achievable the first time.

- **Loyalty focus:** Invite your loyal users to find out more information and make yourself easily available to assist and respond to them.

- **Privacy focus:** When dealing with individuals, e-mail addresses and company information, there's a certain amount of control that is required. At times it is necessary to apply user names and passwords. Be protective, diligent, respectful and very appreciative to these very special customers. ■

Walsh offers special thanks to the Darden Team:
Red Lobster—Jim DeSimone and Joe Chabus
Olive Garden—Steve Coe and& Mara Fayerman
Darden Corporation—Joe Kefauver, Shannon McAleavey, Mike Bernstein, Warren Lombardy, and Patty DeYoung

MEDIA INTERVIEW: JOE ROSENBLOOM OF *INC.*

Joe Rosenbloom is a senior editor for *Inc.* magazine, with 30 years of experience as a journalist. Over the years, Rosenbloom has witnessed the birth of e-mail and the benefits it brings to journalists. In our interview with Rosenbloom, the age-old issue of how PR people communicate improperly with journalists (regardless of pre- or post-Internet) surfaced within the first three minutes of the conversation. Just because e-mail is used as a quick means to deliver information, that doesn't always mean that the information forwarded is accurate or targeted to meet the journalists' audiences. "Even with e-mail, PR people don't make their pitches specific to *Inc.* In most cases, it appears that they don't have enough information about *Inc.*'s stories. And, sometimes they do understand, but don't know how to communicate their knowledge to interest an editor," says Rosenbloom.

Rosenbloom further explained how a PR person can obtain the attention of a journalist (positive and negative) with the following examples:

- Use a subject line that grabs the media's attention. You could put the story idea right in the subject line (although this, too, is becoming common practice). One way to attract attention is to pitch a seasonal story. For instance, when tax season is four months away, the PR person that provides a story idea about tax season right up front in the subject line is likely to get noticed. That's when PR people begin thinking like the editors at the magazine. No longer should PR people use the words "news release" in the subject line. It's overused in general, and, specifically for *Inc.*, it's not relevant, as the magazine does not cover breaking news.

- Be available and knowledgeable on the subject matter should a journalist decide to call for more information. Don't call the journalist to follow up on e-mail. It's a bad habit and the journalist is less likely to use that PR person's information. If the journalist does make the follow-up call, it's imperative that the PR person knows the subject matter and is able to answer a few questions. It's through this conversation that the journalist decides if he or she wants to continue with the story based on the PR person's answers. Remember, an e-mail only gets the attention; the actual human interaction moves the story along. One of Rosenbloom's biggest pet peeves is the person who does not have enough understanding of the company he or she is pitching.

- Use e-mails to accommodate an informational request and provide an instantaneous response. However, as mentioned previously, e-mails do not replace the human interaction with a competent PR professional. Food for thought: Journalists can even detect a lack of confidence or lack of professionalism in an e-mail correspondence.

- Be careful with e-mail and privacy issues. Some journalists are not in favor of being listed with 50 other e-mail addresses on an e-mail list. However, this type of e-mail is becoming more common practice, almost "a part of life." It could be construed as the same principle as seeing the names of editors on a masthead of a publication (it's public knowledge). However, when an editor's e-mail address appears on a long list, the recipient automatically knows that he or she is one of many covering a story, and, therefore, might not pursue the story as if it were an exclusive.

Rosenbloom ended the interview with an interesting story. When asked about the relationships and interactions with PR professionals, one unique instance came to mind. Harvard Business School had contacted *Inc.* to write a story that discussed the undertakings of ambitious entrepreneurship. Rosenbloom pointed out that the PR executive at Harvard Business School was extremely knowledgeable, approached the magazine with credible and relevant information, and knew how to communicate with a journalist properly. One factor that made this person stand out in Rosenbloom's mind was that he never sent one single e-mail correspondence. Therefore, e-mail is definitely a means to enhance a relationship with its true genius (speed), but e-mail is certainly not the basis for a relationship even in the 21st Century. ■

MEDIA INTERVIEW: SCOTT JASCHIK OF *THE CHRONICLE OF HIGHER EDUCATION*

The Chronicle of Higher Education is a privately owned newsweekly serving a paid subscription base of more than 90,000 college professors and administrators. It is an Internet pioneer that has won awards for its own Web site, while carefully chronicling in print and online how the technology has changed how colleges do business.

Editor Scott Jaschik, a 17-year *Chronicle* veteran, says the steady stream of news releases from the more than 3,000 colleges in the United States now flows primarily through e-mail. He and other editors struggle to keep up with the messages because they're always on the lookout for timely stories to report on The Chronicle's Web site at *chronicle.com* in its daily e-mail news service. "I read the tops of them," Jaschik says. "If it's not a good lead, I'm hitting Delete."

Jaschik says his job would be easier if PR representatives actually mentioned the news in the subject line of the e-mail. Something like "$100M gift to U. of X" is much better than a subject line of "U. of X," he notes. "That would certainly affect the speed with which I read it."

Like many journalists, Jaschik prefers to get releases through e-mail so he can see them whether he's in the office or on the road. He can also quickly forward them to writers who might be distant from the newspaper's Washington, DC, headquarters. He is surprised, though, by how many faxes and how much snail mail still flow into his office—containing precisely the same releases that he has already seen in e-mail. "Somewhere out there in PR land, there's a myth that the more ways you send it the better," he says.

Jaschik has praise for the AScribe Newswire, an Internet-based group that circulates the press releases of the nonprofit organizations that comprise its membership. However, he notes that many universities that use AScribe also send the same releases out directly to *The Chronicle*, duplicating the number of incoming e-mails for reporters.

The bottom line, he notes, is the same as it was before the age of the Internet. Reporters are going to pay more attention to pitches that are customized to the interests of their publication. A PR person who takes the time in an e-mail to suggest how the accompanying news might be used in a particular section or feature of the newspaper is going to get more attention than another pitch-maker who demonstrates no familiarity with the publication, Jaschik says. The people who make that kind of effort, he says, are "a minority." ■

8 E-Newsletters Build Relationships

➤ Opt-in newsletters help create relationships with journalists.
➤ E-mail alerts can be easy to set up and operate.
➤ HTML newsletters let you offer richer content, but require more work.

We talked in the last chapter about how e-mail was misused in the Internet's early days by many PR people who saw it as a cheap way to reach hundreds, sometimes thousands, of reporters with a single message. Experience has taught us all that the Internet is not a broadcast medium. Those who fill inboxes with unsolicited, untargeted pitches are derided as spammers and imperil the reputations of themselves and their clients. E-mail is instead a great tool for relationship building with small groups of journalists who can be reached quickly with news related to their particular interests. Getting the news out quickly with an informative subject line is extremely important when it comes to breaking news, as we discussed in Chapter 7. In this chapter, we talk about the growing popularity of periodic newsletters that PR people can distribute to keep reporters in touch with their clients regardless of whether there's big breaking news to report.

Our experience has been that the phrase "electronic newsletter" is frequently used to describe two very different kinds of PR products that have accompanied the growth of the Internet. The more common format is what we refer to as "e-mail alerts," which offer immediate notification of news releases to reporters who have registered for the service. The alerts save reporters from having to search PR Newswire or Business Wire for the latest releases of companies on their beats. Another benefit is that many companies offer the alerts in selected categories, so that reporters can subscribe to only the ones that relate to their particular beats, such as financial data, or to particular product segments like home computing or enterprise computing. The second type of newsletter is a bit more sophisticated and, therefore, more rare. Its goal is not to win coverage of the latest announcement, but to keep reporters informed of the company's product offerings and market position and to build the reputations of its executives as industry experts. Some of the better ones we've seen resemble in many ways the types of newsletters that large companies have circulated to employees for decades. They try to explain recent news events in the context of the company's overall mission. Because an external newsletter for reporters doesn't need to provide updates on how to file HMO claims, for example, there is plenty of screen space left for features like "upcoming events," which can advise reporters of scheduled earnings announcements, executives' speeches, or trade show appearances.

E-MAIL ALERTS

E-mail alerts are the most common type of opt-in newsletter for public relations because they are relatively easy to set up and administer. A company can announce the launch of an alert service at the bottom of every press release it issues and direct reporters to a sign-up page on the Web. The sign-up process can be automated to collect e-mail addresses and to ask the journalist which categories of releases he or she would like to receive. In some cases, the reporter is asked to choose a password that can be used to return to the sign-up page to change his or her category preferences or to unsubscribe to the alert service.

Among the companies that offer e-mail alerts is Procter & Gamble, which had a link in its online pressroom labeled "Press Release Signup" when we last checked. Reporters who click the link and then type in their name and e-mail address on the Web page are signed up for P&G News, which provides immediate e-mailed copies of all P&G press releases when they are added to the company's Web site. Reporters can return to the same Web page to unsubscribe to P&G News.

Another alert sender is computer chip maker Intel, which features its Intel Newswire service prominently in the company's online pressroom. A reporter provides an e-mail address and picks a password and then selects from a list of about three dozen topics that includes everything from General Corporate News to Mobile Computing. The selection of releases can be limited further by listing one or more keywords that must be included in a release for it to be sent to the reporter. Finally, the reporter is asked to tell Intel how frequently he or she would like to receive the e-mailed releases. They can be sent immediately when they are posted to Intel's online pressroom or all appropriate releases can be bundled and sent on a daily or weekly basis. The differences in frequency enable reporters who do not cover breaking news to avoid being inundated with Intel releases. A daily or weekly package might indeed be preferable for a reporter at a weekly or monthly publication who isn't writing about every announcement, but just wants to keep in touch with what is happening at a market leader such as Intel.

Ken Statham of Intel's press relations office says the Newswire is automated, so it does not place any extra burdens on the PR staff. Each release just needs to be tagged for distribution to the appropriate category or categories. The automated nature of it means that it hasn't been difficult to serve large numbers of recipients. "We have thousands of subscribers and expect to eventually have tens of thousands," says Statham. "However, boosting the number of subscribers is not our objective. Our goal is to provide convenience for our press/analyst customers."

Things are a little less simple at Cornell University, where Bill Steele manages electronic products for the university's news service. Cornell provides students and employees with access to Listserv software, which can be used to administer mailing lists. However, the actual task of creating the lists for Cornell's news service and uploading press releases falls to Steele, a science writer and self-taught programmer. Steele has created 16 lists over the last six years that provide recipients with releases related to particular academic fields, such as social sciences, the arts, or law. Steele has written a script that enables him to tag each release as it is posted on the Web and have it automatically sent out as an e-mail to subscribers of a particular list. He's also written a script for managing returned e-mail and he jokes that whoever replaces him will have a tough time figuring out his system. (For more on how Steele manages Cornell's newsletters, see our interview with him on page 116 in this chapter.)

INFORMATION-RICH NEWSLETTERS

Most people in public relations are probably well aware that e-newsletters can be much more powerful and useful than just automated alerts. Many of us subscribe to newsletters created by journalism organizations ranging from *The Wall Street Journal* to Internet.com that help us stay on top of breaking news stories.

Our point here is that PR people can create e-newsletters on their own that are just as attractive as the journalism-oriented newsletters and that can be helpful in getting more attention for our clients. E-mail alerts are nice to make sure your big release is well read, but why not use the power of HTML newsletters to provide reporters monthly or quarterly insights into how your client views its markets and what its top executives have to say about industry announcements and events?

Examples of PR-produced e-newsletters are still rare, but they provide us with some insights into what is needed for success. Because reporters already feel inundated with e-mail, they're not likely to be interested in receiving e-mail newsletters unless they are persuaded that the offering amounts to more than regurgitated press releases. What they want from the newsletter is some analysis of industry events that will help them do their jobs better. "We need to get reporters to read what we send them because they know it's good stuff," says Elizabeth Albrycht, a partner in Albrycht McClure & Partners, a PR firm that's a proponent of e-newsletters.

These demands for truly useful information mean that e-newsletters are not a task for the weak of heart in public relations. Someone needs to be developing content on a regular basis and going through the effort of signing up reporters and managing an opt-in list. We also think it's fine to supplement the main features with the kinds of things we've recommended for your online pressrooms: a list of recent press mentions, a digest of recent releases, and a calendar of upcoming events and trade shows. These newsletter features can simply be links to the appropriate pages in your online pressroom, but their presence in the newsletter makes recipients aware of where your company has been featured and what it is planning in the way of future events.

Given a newsletter's demand for original, analytical copy, it's not surprising that some of the better e-newsletters we've seen have come from consulting firms. Because the newsletter can be a strong tool for establishing yourself as an industry expert, it's also not surprising that some of the earliest e-newsletters have popped up in emerging industries with no recognized experts. One industry, in particular, in which newsletters have proliferated is in mobile computing, a sector that aims to bring business applications and Internet connections to cell phones, personal digital assistants (PDAs), and other devices. Several trade publishers have newsletters in this field. Makers of cell phones and PDAs have also jumped into the fray with newsletters for their customers and trade press. Web sites created to sell wireless devices have offered newsletters as a way of building relationships with prospective customers.

One entrant that impressed us and won praise from many reporters is M-Insights from Mobilocity, a consulting firm launched in 1999 with the mission of helping companies plan their use of wireless data devices. The firm was absorbed into Qualcomm's Wireless Knowledge unit in 2002 and the newsletter was discontinued. It had been developed by Miller Shandwick in conjunction with the analysts at Mobilocity, and employed a "just the facts" approach that featured quick, pithy commentary on recent industry events. The format featured a brief synopsis of a recent announcement and then an "Our Take" segment in which Mobilocity told readers what it thought of the announcement.

In one example, the M-Insights newsletter dated August 30, 2001 reported on an initiative by Palm Inc., maker of the Palm Pilot, to help develop applications for real estate professionals. In its commentary, Mobilocity pointed out the broader story to reporters by asserting that mobile devices like Palm Pilots and other PDAs offer many mobile professionals in real estate, health care, and other fields their first real opportunity to benefit from information technology because they were never well served by PC applications intended to be used in an office.

Another feature in the M-Insights newsletter was called M-Spotlight, and it enabled Mobilocity to portray itself as a voice of authority. The feature was frequently used to list principles that should be followed in developing m-commerce applications and to highlight successful efforts of Mobilocity's clients. As part of the M-Insights newsletter, these reports were easier to read than the typical case study press release and they helped to portray the companies involved as m-commerce pioneers.

Anne Coyle of Weber Shandwick, who helped to launch M-Insights while at Miller Shandwick, says the newsletter's approach was a successful one. "M-Insights helped us to gain mind-share in a crowded marketplace," she notes. "Our goal was to get them to rise above the noise where they could show what they knew," she adds. The newsletter "fit very much into the consulting model of look at what's going on, gather facts, and make an analysis."

For all of its success, however, M-Insights also pointed out some pitfalls to be careful of when undertaking a newsletter. Launched as a weekly, M-Insights became biweekly and later monthly primarily because it became difficult to keep it stocked with high-quality content. As the consulting business took off, the consultants had less time for the newsletter, Coyle says. "No one really owned it," she laments. "You have to have someone who's going to own it and really run with it." (For more on Coyle's experience with Mobilocity, see our interview with her on page 117 in this chapter.)

Albrycht McClure & Partners, a PR firm with many startup companies as clients, believes that an e-newsletter is a smart tool for reaching a number of constituencies, including the press, employees, potential investors, and prospective business partners. Clients with limited staff can make a single effort to develop a newsletter that meets the needs of the various constituencies, says Elizabeth Albrycht. The newsletter can be built around a template to keep production costs down, she says, but the client must be willing to invest mindpower. "You want to have some strong writers and thinkers on this," she says.

Albrycht McClure & Partners thinks a newsletter would be especially effective for companies in emerging fields. Albrycht notes that her firm had success promoting a small company called InfiniCon Systems by taking an unorthodox approach in press releases in which it offered 10 questions that network administrators should be asking themselves about network architectures. "It was a real stretch doing what we were doing with releases," she says, noting that an e-newsletter would be a much more appropriate vehicle for educating reporters and prospective customers about a new technology.

Albrycht notes that a good e-newsletter can bring more people to a client's Web site and expose them to the online pressroom and other offerings. However, she notes that this feature cuts both ways in that the newsletter must be carefully coordinated with the Web site so that newsletter recipients actually find what they are seeking on the Web site. This cooperation can be difficult if the PR people are not responsible for Web site operations, she notes. "Doing these types of things does require more rigor on the part of the client," she says. (For more on what Albrycht and partner Jennifer McClure have to say about e-newsletters, see our interview with them on page 119 in this chapter.)

One feature we haven't seen in e-newsletters, but believe could be useful and popular with journalists, is a regular feature highlighting the opinions of your client's top executives. We think a quotable CEO who is willing to speak candidly about the company's latest news or about the latest activities of its competitors could really shine in a newsletter column. He or she might talk about current topics; for example, how the company responded to the events of September 11 or how it is helping to revitalize an inner-city school. The right CEO might even offer his or her review of the latest management tome topping the bestseller charts. The idea is to make the newsletter's recipients feel they are getting a look at "the real CEO" beyond the boilerplate quotes that appear in press releases. He or she does not need to be outrageous to attract media interest. Remember, each newsletter is not supposed to spawn a certain number of stories, but rather it is intended to extend the company's relationship with the journalist and possibly lead to more references to your CEO as a voice of authority, veteran manager, renaissance figure, philanthropist, and so on. Be careful, however. A boring CEO with nothing to say could torpedo the whole newsletter if he or she contributes lame columns that focus on how this quarter's EBITDA compares to that of the same quarter last year.

DOS AND DON'TS

We cannot overemphasize the importance of getting the journalists to opt in for your newsletter, a process that will undoubtedly reduce the number of recipients below what you think it should be. Remember, however, sending something to people who do not want to read it is not going to give them a good impression of you, your agency, or your client. You should think of the opt-in requirement as a handshake with the reporter in which you are agreeing to have a relationship and you are consenting to deliver newsletters containing useful information. You should make new subscribers confirm their interest in your newsletter by going to a Web page and checking a box or by replying to your initial mailing. Without this confirmation step, you could have people unknowingly signed up for your newsletter by friends or enemies. You must also make it easy for the reporter to unsubscribe from your newsletter by either responding to your e-mail with an unsubscribe request or by including a URL where the recipient can go to unsubscribe.

More standards for administering newsletters can be found at *mail-abuse.org*, and similar sites administered by antispam groups. These groups should be taken seriously because they are generally supported by Internet service providers (ISPs) who could opt to block all e-mail from your company if they feel your company is operating a newsletter without adequate controls.

One of us knows from personal experience as a former editor of a daily newsletter for *Internet World* magazine of the importance of keeping the spam police happy with your organization. In one case, an opt-in subscriber who had difficulty reaching the URL that *Internet World* provided for unsubscribe requests filed a complaint with the spam police. It turned out that the e-mail distribution company responsible for the unsubscribe Web page had moved it to a different server and neglected to change the URL listed in *Internet World*'s newsletter. The problem was quickly remedied, but not before the police organization had gone to the ISP that housed *Internet World*'s Web site and urged it to dump *Internet World* as a customer. A flurry of phone calls was needed to keep the Web site online and to explain the situation to the spam police. In another incident, *Internet World*'s e-mail distribution company introduced a stray character in the message ID when it was sending out the newsletter. An undetermined number of ISPs began rejecting the newsletter because of the anomaly. This type of problem is particularly dangerous to the newsletter publisher because no one calls to warn you. Instead, the number of bouncebacks rose unexpectedly and the distributor started an investigation that seemed to go nowhere until a loyal newsletter reader investigated the absence of the newsletter with her ISP and was told that it was being blocked as possible spam.

Our point is to tread carefully. If you're going to put a lot of time and effort into creating a first-class newsletter, make sure you're following established practices for distributing it. You want the newsletter to bring you accolades, not accusations.

In our next chapter, we discuss the appropriate uses of Webcasts and other technologies that you might be considering for reaching out to the press and to consumers.

PR INTERVIEW:
BILL STEELE OF CORNELL NEWS SERVICE

Bill Steele doesn't remember Cornell's move to e-mail alerts as a bold step forward for public relations at the Ivy League university. Instead, he says, he was asked to make a paper-based digest of press releases available online because the university thought it might save some money on postage.

Steele says he put together a Web page for signing up for the "Science Tips" digest and he established a mailing list using the Listserv software that Cornell runs on its computers for the benefit of any student or employee who wishes to administer an e-mail–based discussion group. Six years later, Steele administers 16 different lists offering recipients press releases tailored to their interests in areas such as life sciences, the arts, law, and veterinary medicine. "There's a couple thousand subscribed to something," says Steele, noting that the lists have attracted not only journalists, but also Cornell students, alumni, and other people with an interest in academic research.

Steele created a system of categories for sorting stories onto the Cornell News Service Web pages and those categories correspond to the various e-mail newsletter lists. He wrote a script that takes each story that is posted to the Web pages and automatically sends it out as an e-mail to those people who have signed up for the corresponding e-mail list.

The process is not completely automated, Steele says, noting that it still requires a human to put each press release into the appropriate subject categories. Because one of the lists is a digest of press releases that carries only the first two paragraphs of each release, a sharp eye is needed to ensure that the reader has been given the gist of the story in the two opening paragraphs.

The Listserv software takes a lot of work out of the distribution process, but Steele notes that he still has to deal with a handful of undeliverable messages every time a mailing goes out. He has written a script that actually keeps track of delivery problems and deletes recipients from lists after three consecutive delivery errors.

Steele says he believes the press release lists serve the needs of the reporters using Cornell News Service and so he's not rushing into HTML newsletters or anything more sophisticated or bandwidth intensive. "I wouldn't want to do that because there are still an awful lot of people downloading this over the phone," he says. "I don't want to use all of the bells and whistles all the time." ■

PR INTERVIEW: ANNE COYLE OF WEBER SHANDWICK

Anne Coyle says the e-mail newsletter represented the best tool for making more people aware of Mobilocity, a consulting firm that launched in 1999 with the mission of helping customers develop plans for mobile computing. Each week a new M-Insights newsletter offered the four founders of Mobilocity a chance to show off their expertise by analyzing the latest announcements in the field and their anticipated impact on the development of applications for PDAs, cell phones, and other wireless devices. "It fit very much into the consulting model of look at what's going on, gather facts, and make an analysis," she says.

Coyle says M-Insights also worked because Mobilocity was a hard-charging startup with people eager to put in the extra work needed for the newsletter. Many of the early employees were fresh from college and were used to meeting deadlines and working on projects collaboratively. The founders understood that the newsletter was a way to get noticed and to influence the way journalists were thinking about an emerging field that was full of more hype than facts. "Our goal was to get them to rise above the noise," she says. "They could show what they knew."

Coyle says the success of M-Insights, or any other newsletter, is difficult to measure because you're not serving up a story that produces a specific number of press mentions. "It's tough to measure, but you know when it's working well," she says. The biggest tipoff, she says, is that the newsletter starts generating questions and comments from reporters and other recipients. "Sometimes they didn't agree with our take," Coyle remembers. "But at that point we were happy to have the response."

She notes that Mobilocity was always careful to avoid making M-Insights look like a sales vehicle of any kind. The goal, she explains, was to get recipients to think, "This is research coming out of a company—not anything too slick or commercialized."

The collaborative authorship of M-Insights, which helped infuse it with enthusiasm in its early weeks, later became something of a problem, Coyle says, because no one person was in charge of the newsletter. As Mobilocity took on more clients, analysts on the staff were too busy to contribute as much for the newsletter, which started coming out less frequently, first on a biweekly basis and then on a monthly basis. "You have to have someone who's going to own it and really run with it," she says. The newsletter died after Mobilocity became part of Qualcomm's Wireless Knowledge unit in 2002.

M-Insights was never aesthetically flashy, Coyle says, noting that it was available in plain text and in a version with fonts that worked best with Palm Pilots and other devices. Recipients are less concerned with how something looks than they are with the quality of the information it contains, and M-Insights effectively met the needs of a relatively small group of journalists and technologists who were all trying to figure out how mobile computing would be used in the business world. "You really want to hit the right people," says Coyle. "That's where PR works at its best."

Coyle counsels others who may be planning newsletters to abide by opt-in practices, rather than just sending the bulky e-mail to everyone on your press list. Many people who get newsletters to which they haven't subscribed are going to hold it against the sender, which could negatively affect their coverage of your client, she says. When people sign up for the newsletter, you should tell them how their names and e-mail addresses will be used and you should constantly remind them of how they can unsubscribe, she says.

One downside of publishing an electronic newsletter, Coyle notes, is that your product is easily excerpted and reproduced and sometimes held up for ridicule on message boards. Your client, who is helping to write the newsletter, needs to be thick-skinned enough to tolerate a certain amount of vitriol from strongly opinionated Internet users. "You've lost control once you've hit Send," says Coyle. ■

Albrycht McClure & Partners is a virtual public relations and marketing agency that believes enough in the future of electronic newsletters that it offers a quarterly newsletter as one of its four core service offerings. The firm, which is headed jointly by Elizabeth Albrycht in northern Virginia and Jennifer McClure in northern California, says it will help clients develop, edit, and publish newsletters four times a year for a fee of $5,000. That's the same fee as the firm charges for producing a press kit and slightly less than the $6,000 it charges to handle trade show briefings and materials. Its most expensive package starts at $10,000 for everything that goes into a product announcement.

Both partners admit, however, that they haven't exactly been flooded with requests for e-newsletters. "It's something new to think about, certainly from a traditional PR perspective," says Albrycht. However, they're optimistic that the newsletter will fill an important place between the press release and the informal e-mail sent to keep reporters up to date. "This gives us a nice tool to take to the CEO whose reaction is usually "Do a press release,'" she says. "Usually, they're not happy with an e-mail," she adds. "Executives like this because it's more formal."

Reporters, meanwhile, will like the newsletter if it's useful, Albrycht says. This means it needs to talk about issues in a substantive way, she says. "We need to get reporters to read what we send them because they know it's good stuff," she says.

Albrycht and McClure believe the work they've done for a technology company called InfiniCon Systems would slide nicely into an e-newsletter. Their approach in a series of press releases has been to identify and answer major questions that network administrators (and trade press reporters) have about new network architectures. The tone has been "very vendor-neutral," Albrycht says, and yet it has produced press inquiries, beta customers for InfiniCon's technology, and prospective employees and business partners for the company. "It was a real stretch doing what we were doing with these releases," says Albrycht. "We really think the e-newsletter is the tool of the future."

Albrycht says she thinks e-newsletters are particularly attractive to startup companies, which are trying to serve many constituencies, including the press, potential investors, and prospective customers. Rather than having a small staff stretched thin to work on different materials for each constituency, staff members can work collaboratively on an e-newsletter that meets the needs of all the constituent groups.

Newsletters, however, are not easy to assemble, Albrycht notes. "You want to have some strong writers and thinkers on this," she says. "Every six weeks is probably the most often that we'll do it," she says, noting the need to always have content planned out well in advance for every issue.

You also need the cooperation of the client in developing the content and in coordinating what's in the newsletter with what's on the client's Web site, Albrycht says. In most cases, you want the newsletter to contain the start of a story before offering a link to the full story on the client's Web site, she says. You also want the client to be tracking the activities of the newsletter readers when they arrive on the site, she notes. This can be done by directing readers to the site through a URL that is only publicized in the newsletter. "It gives you a richer sense of what people are thinking and what they're interested in," she says.

Albrycht says she has enough confidence in the quality of her press and analyst lists that she'd feel comfortable sending an e-newsletter to those lists and providing recipients with an opportunity to opt out of future mailings. Her partner, Jennifer McClure, concurs in this judgment. "We should know the right people," she says, noting that the maximum number of recipients would never be more than "a couple hundred" because the lists are so targeted.

McClure says such targeted mailings can be handled in-house, rather than shipped out to e-mail distribution companies like DoubleClick or CheetahMail. Adding and deleting addresses, changing addresses, and handling undelivered mail is not a huge task, she says. "It's a couple hours of busy work that our admin staff can do."

Questions and comments from newsletter readers should be routed to a real person, rather than a general catch-all e-mail address, McClure says, and people should get responses from a human in a timely fashion. After all, she points out, "the key to the success of these newsletters is using them as a tool to build a relationship." ■

MEDIA INTERVIEW: MIKE COHN OF *INTERNET WORLD*

Mike Cohn has been in technology publishing for almost 20 years, starting out at *PC Magazine* and serving stints at *Accounting Technology* and *Beyond Computing*. By the time he came to Penton Media's *Internet World* in 2000, the Internet had dramatically changed the tools of his trade. Snail mail was pretty much useless. Faxes were being overtaken by e-mail. What Cohn did not know was how important e-newsletters were about to become to his job.

A senior editor who specializes in covering the emerging field of mobile computing and m-commerce, Cohn has found a number of e-newsletters invaluable in keeping up with what's happening. The M-Insights newsletter from consulting firm Mobilocity, which has already been discussed in this chapter, helped to shape his view of industry events and build his opinion of Mobilocity's cofounder Omar Javaid as an industry analyst. Other consultant groups have also produced good newsletters, Cohn says, noting Andrew Seybold's Outlook 4Mobility, and newsletter efforts from Zona Research and EMC. "A lot of them repeat the same news," Cohn says, "but you hope they're able to get into insights, comparisons, and context. It also helps when they have a sense of humor."

Cohn says individual companies have also jumped on the newsletter bandwagon. He says the newsletter from Handspring, which makes the Visor handheld device that competes with Palm Pilots, is directed at Visor owners, but has helped him in understanding Handspring's market strategies. One edition of the newsletter included a first-person account of how a woman used a Visor to track her contractions and get herself through labor and childbirth.

Cohn notes that Poet Software, which makes business-to-business software, has also produced newsletters about uses of Java-enabled devices. "I thought that was a good way to get their name out there and provide some value," he says.

He notes that none of the e-newsletters he's received has been graphically beautiful and many are done in simple text to accommodate the users of small devices who are interested in the subject matter but cannot display fancy HTML documents. Newsletters, Cohn says, are much more valuable than the "canned stories" offered in press releases. ■

9 WEBCASTS ARE WORTH A SECOND TRY

➤ Online multimedia presentations—often called Webcasts—enable PR people to control the message.

➤ Putting press conferences and other events online meshes well with widespread concerns about travel costs and safety.

➤ Would-be Webcasters have more technology options than ever before.

Now that we've covered the basics of PR in the Internet age (online newsrooms and e-mail) and the tools that we hope will become more popular (opt-in newsletters), we turn our attention to a fast-growing technology that many readers might have already tried and dismissed. Yes, we're talking about Webcasts, those problem-plagued adventures of 1999 that made video from the space shuttle seem high quality—that is, if you were able to overcome firewall issues and network bottlenecks to even log on.

We suffered along with the rest of you, squeezing our mouses in anger as we tried to join an event at the appointed time only to find out our streaming player was out of date or that the best we could achieve was a jerky image of a speaker with major audio hiccups. However, we're here to encourage all of you to get back on the horse. The buzz about Webcasting might have dissipated in recent years, but the technology has improved, costs have come down, and the world has been changed so dramatically by the economic downturn and the tragedies of September 11, 2001 that Webcasting makes a huge amount of sense for PR professionals.

According to Wainhouse Research's December 2001 User Survey, a tool used to project statistics 12 months out in time, Web conferencing and streaming will see the greatest growth in the services industry. Access to broadband Internet connections is increasing, which enables more customers to log on to Webcasts with ease. In addition, Webcast service providers are offering better ways to build technology for companies to suit specific needs. Research also tells us that Webcasts are becoming more popular and accepted among Internet users. Edison Media Research and Arbitron reported in August 2001 in a Webcasting study that 50 percent more online users have tried streaming media as compared to the audio-only listeners in July 1999. Furthermore, according to the study, over one-third of all Americans age 12 and older are included in a newly named category called "Streamies" encompassing approximately 78 million people.

Ask a handful of PR people about their Webcast experiences and at least a few will recall the first Victoria's Secret Webcast in February 1999, which became a victim of its own huge success. It was so well promoted that too many people logged on at once to check out the models in their sexy lingerie. From the start of the event, it took the average person longer than two-and-a-half minutes to download the Web page as compared to the normal one-minute time frame to which Victoria's Secret customers had been accustomed. A Web tracking company reported the number of visitors to the Victoria's Secret's site reached approximately 1.5 million during the fashion show, but for many of those visitors the Webcast was a disappointment. The technical difficulties also threatened to overshadow the lingerie in the press coverage of the Webcast.

Indeed, the danger of public embarrassment is what seems to concern PR professionals the most when weighing the merits of Webcasting. It's difficult enough for PR people to deal with the daily interactions of their brands with customers, shareholders, analysts, the media, and all stakeholders of a company online and offline. Why take more chances deliberately with the brand's reputation? If you've ever planned an event, then surely you know it's hairy enough with the normal planning, coordinating, and implementing of the program. Should we add temperamental technology to the list of potential issues? We say, "Yes." We believe you would be doing a disservice to your brand if you didn't try to communicate to audiences who can log on to the Internet, who need to hear from the brand, and who would not interact with the brand otherwise (i.e., those who can't be physically present for an event that communicates an important message). Perhaps the best support for our opinion comes from Victoria's Secret itself, which was still Webcasting the last time that we checked. Its second event in May 2000 attracted more than 2 million viewers and proved easier to access thanks to technical help the company enlisted from Akamai, IBM, Microsoft, and Yahoo!.

Our positive feelings about Webcasting are also influenced by the examples of Webcasts we've seen in recent months and by our conversations with providers of Webcasting services. One big fan of the technology is Larry Weber, chairman and CEO of Interpublic's Advanced Marketing Services, which includes Weber Shandwick Worldwide, Golin/Harris International, and DeVries Public Relations. A Webcasting pioneer, he tried out the technology with some success as early as 1996 for clients such as 3Com and U.S. Robotics when each production cost as much as $30,000. Costs have come down and Interpublic ramped up to more than 300 Webcasts in 2001, Weber says, explaining that he sees the technology as a key to the emergence of what he calls "visual PR." Pubic relations professionals can use this technology to tell their clients' stories in visually appealing ways without interference from journalists. "The PR department of the future is going to have creative directors, and partners in multimedia," he says. "It's going to be a different kind of approach and it's going to be visually driven."

We agree with Weber and see his vision starting to become reality as more PR agencies learn to adopt creative approaches to the Web and also take the time to work closely with IT departments to align PR and Web communications. We believe that Weber's notion of visual PR will add credibility to a brand as visual presentations are more dynamic, audience reach is broader, and online viewers feel closer to the brand by viewing a Webcast delivered directly to their PCs. It's time for PR folks to pay more attention to visual PR and to become more aware, educated, comfortable, and well-spoken regarding the use of Webcasts and the strategies needed to implement them successfully.

An important step in the learning process is to determine when it is necessary to use a Webcast. The technology became hot years ago as part of the hype that surrounded the Internet and the accompanying belief in spending incredibly large amounts of money to move simple offline traditions like press conferences into the Internet age. However, that pursuit overlooked the power of canned Webcasts—brief video productions that tell your client's story in a format that can be retrieved over and over again by numerous viewers at times that are most convenient for them. One of our favorite examples of archiving a Webcast video production can be found on JVC's National Association of Broadcasters (NAB) Web site. The site was developed by Deirdre Breakenridge's agency to allow JVC's audiences (the media and JVC's customers) who could not attend the NAB trade show to be thoroughly involved and well informed through this Web site. In conjunction with JVC's new Streamcorder professional camcorder (the GY-DV300), which has streaming capabilities to the Web, JVC was able to capture its entire booth exhibit online, complete with demos, executive speeches, and presentations. When JVC visitors logged onto the site they could preregister if they were attending the trade show and print out a coupon for a free T-shirt, or sign up to receive e-mail alerts to notify them that there was streaming video available to enjoy. The creation of the JVC NAB site was an excellent strategy to keep JVC's audiences informed with the same information they would have received if they were able to travel to Las Vegas for the four-day event. The ability to Webcast produced the outcome of well-informed audiences and a company that satisfied both trade show attendees and nonattendees.

Pat Meier, who runs her own PR agency in Mill Valley, California, is a former broadcast journalist who believes strongly in the power of prerecorded Webcasts. "By Webcasting, you actually are your own medium," she says, noting the PR person's ability to control everything from the editing and backdrop for the video to the makeup and clothing of the executive chosen to represent his or her client. The Webcast gives the PR person more control over the message the client seeks to deliver than would ever be possible through an appearance on a local TV business show or even on CNBC, she notes. (For more on Meier's use of Webcasts, see our interview with her on page 141 in this chapter.)

We certainly agree that canned Webcasts are worth pursuing as a component of the online pressrooms we encouraged you to develop in Chapter 6. A number of major universities, for example, feature welcome messages from their presidents on their Web sites, enabling each institution to portray its president in the most flattering light. Major companies, such as Air Product & Chemicals, also feature video in their online pressrooms as we discussed in Chapter 6 as a means of explaining exactly what it is that their companies do.

LIVE EVENTS

For many people, however, the term *Webcast* is used primarily to describe a live event that they are seeking to make available to a larger audience by taking it onto the Web. It can certainly be argued that interest in such events has risen since the tragedies of September 11, 2001, as it's become more difficult to get investors, customers, employees, and the media to travel to large events. The economic recession also works in favor of Webcasts because many companies have tightened up on travel expenses and slashed jobs—leaving the remaining workers with less time to travel.

PR people who investigate Webcasting will find a large variety of options that go beyond the full-fledged option favored by Victoria's Secret. PR professionals can bring together corporate officers, the media, stockholders, and other stakeholders in a company through an array of formats encompassing everything from audio-only events to audio-enhanced slide shows, to live video events that allow one-way announcements or two-way interaction over the phone, via e-mail, or in chat rooms for limited amounts of time. Often the Webcasts are stored on the company's Web site where they can be accessed on demand for weeks and months to come by reporters and other interested parties.

Different formats work best for different needs. Many in the investor relations community say that audio-only Webcasts or audio-enhanced slide shows are generally sufficient for quarterly earnings reports when it is more important to see charts and graphs on the slides than to see a talking head behind a podium. On the other hand, a new product announcement might be handled best on a video Webcast in which you want to display the product and capture the enthusiasm of the company's product managers and executives.

We asked Terri Walters, president and CEO of Moonfish Production, an event production management firm in New Jersey, to walk us through the steps she follows in helping her clients determine what types of Webcasts are appropriate for them. As an event producer, she sees Webcasts as a great enhancement to provide to her clients. Although much improved over recent years, Walters still sees Webcasts as being in their infancy with a huge amount of potential as they improve. Webcasts will evolve so that people in rural residential areas will have better connections to participate and dial-up connections will no longer be an issue that restricts audience participation. PR people need to be ready now to deliver programs as cable modems and DSL bring more people into the broadband age.

The first thing that Walters likes to tell PR people is that Webcasts are not a cheap means to an end. Luckily, the $30,000 Webcasts experienced by Weber in 1996 are not always the case today. In 2002, costs for a Webcast with an audio and video presentation ranged between $5,000 and $10,000.

Walters advises many professionals on whether or not they need a Webcast. There are many factors that determine if a Webcast is necessary, including accessibility of the audience, how best to communicate, budget, and so on. If the company has the budget, then Walters offers the following checklist of questions for assistance in determining the right kind of event:

- Who will log on to the Internet to view the event?
- What is the proposed venue for the Webcast?
- Is the venue a learning environment?
- Is the event a simple Webcast with no audience participation or is it an interactive online conference?
- Should the Webcast be shot in the office environment?
- Is the engineering location of the Webcast able to support the necessary bandwidth requirements?
- Are there firewall issues that would hinder access to the Webcast?
- Is there a camcorder available to handle the direct video feed and audio feed?

In addition to answering these questions, PR professionals need to know how a company should technically prepare itself in other ways to deliver a successful Webcast. The old saying "What you put into it is what you get out of it" certainly applies here. Walters provided a few things to remember for PR professionals working with an event production firm:

- Light speakers properly. Under- or overlighting will blur your image.
- Check background colors and settings to optimize readability for the viewing audience.
- Restrain camera movement to provide a clearer image.
- Use PowerPoint slides, along with the video presentation to reinforce the message.
- Incorporate live links and live chats to encourage audience participation.
- Use "lower thirds" (i.e., the speaker's name) and the company logo in the Webcast to "ID" the entire event.

Once all of the general questions are answered and the technical issues resolved, Walters finds that implementing the event is the easy—and fun—part. She noted that if the production company does its job properly, it is that much easier for the PR people, who have enough issues to deal with when coordinating and implementing an event of this nature.

PR people who opt to work without a production company have a variety of options when it comes to finding a company to handle the technical aspects of delivering the Webcast. We've found that several large companies are investing in the ability to provide Webcasting services. When Yahoo! announced the launch of Webcasting solutions in September 2001 and PR Newswire climbed aboard in conjunction with Thomson Financial, new credibility was added to the pro side of the Webcasting argument. Yahoo!, a company very much in tune with the needs of Web consumer and business audiences, now offers what the company refers to as "corporate communications solutions." According to Yahoo! the company's announcement responds to the increasing demand for business services that are alternatives to traditional communications. With its Virtual Conference and Executive Communications Center offerings, Yahoo!'s Broadcast (*broadcast.yahoo.com*) unit provides new choices for conferences, trade shows, and sales meetings. Yahoo!'s Virtual Conference is designed to offer interested companies the ability to have audio, video, and informational slides incorporated in an online Webcasting presentation. With Yahoo!'s Virtual Conference Center, a company can select whether an event is live or archived for on-demand use. In addition, document sharing and the ability to have an online Q&A session incorporated into the Webcast event are other interactive options. Audience tracking and surveys are also a necessary part of measuring the outcome of the event, and Yahoo! makes it easy for companies to take full advantage of this option. Yahoo!'s Executive Communications Center offering is a little different from its Virtual Conference. This offering is otherwise known as a Breaking News Channel and is used for quick internal company communication for the delivery of critical or "high-level" time-sensitive knowledge. According to Jim Fanella, senior vice president of Yahoo!'s Business and Enterprise Services Division, the power to reach hundreds to thousands of people is imperative to strategic business communications. Yahoo! has launched the tools to better facilitate the delivery of critical information to every group a company needs to reach, from customers and sales forces to business partners and the media.

PR Newswire has been servicing public relations professionals for years and is well known for its tremendous reach and distribution of news to thousands of media outlets. When a company like PR Newswire teams up with a company like Thomson Financial, known for its technology solutions, the result is a host of Webcasting services with wide-reaching media distribution that far surpasses what either company could achieve alone. (See our interview with Michelle Savage, vice president of investor relations services, and Mark DeLaurentis, divisional vice president of eventcasting at MultiVu, a PR Newswire company, on pages 138 and 139 in this chapter.)

Another interesting company we interviewed is Netbriefings (*netbriefings.com*), which is known for its worldwide online conferencing services. Headquartered in St. Paul, Minnesota, the company offers a convenient, easy, and less costly way to develop events online to educate larger audiences. In addition, with an easy Event Management System, Netbriefings' clients learn how to develop and design their own events specifically for the Web, including creation of event templates, through a simple Web-browser–based interface. Gary Anderson, president and CEO of Netbriefings, told us about the company's array of services. Netbriefings offers Webcasting solutions from the high-end full studio and audio event to midrange PowerPoint presentations with streaming video. The company also provides lower level Webcasts that include PowerPoint presentations with audio conferences.

What stands out the most from our conversation with Anderson is the amount of work his company does with public relations professionals as well as event and convention planners. He feels that his company is working with PR professionals who represent many different industries involved with online events from the Office of the United States Trade Representative and its 4th Ministerial Conference of the World Trade Organization (WTO) in Saudi Arabia to St. Paul-based Lawson Software for its CUE 2001 annual user conference. The Webcast from Saudi Arabia is an excellent example of an event that occurred after September 11, 2001, in which the delegates from many large multinational corporations were unable to travel to that region of the world. Many simply did not want to make the trip and the Webcast brought the delegates to an online community to accomplish their communication objectives with unprecedented access to this event. This particular event was incredibly valuable in that it allowed the Webcast of a high-profile event with news and information reaching those involved even prior to newspapers and major networks disseminating the information. Netbriefings' Webcast of Lawson Software's CUE 2001 conference was another successful event that illustrated the increasing interest among companies in Webcasting for public relations events. The press conference, which is held every year in Anaheim, California, is a forum to announce new products and emphasize customer success stories. With high-tech public relations being extremely competitive in recent years, media coverage and physical attendance at these events have failed to meet expectations. The ability to Webcast a news conference and then archive video on demand with electronic press kits is an excellent way to accommodate editors and reporters whose schedules do not permit event attendance. With respect to Lawson's Webcast conference Anderson stated, "We are pleased to have innovative, high-tech clients, like Lawson Software, adopting our technology for innovative uses that demonstrate benefits beyond those for which we are recognized."

Anderson also discussed several other issues regarding Webcasts that should pique the interest of PR professionals. They, too, attest to the fact that Webcasts are on the rise, just based on Netbriefings' increase in business. In August 2001, Netbriefings was only receiving a few hits a day on its Web site, but that figure has gone up dramatically since then, as have the requests for information or live demos of the company's Webcast solutions. The market has changed a great deal as Web conferencing has become larger, and is expected to become a $5.2 billion market in 2005. Anderson believes that Netbriefings' success with Webcasts and its ability to service so many different companies has to do with the level of customer service and consulting that the company provides. Webcasting has its share of issues and Netbriefings is right on top of three very important issues to ensure they do not pose any problems moving forward:

- Bandwidth: Netbriefings works to determine end-user audiences. If it's a corporate audience, is there a DSL or T1 line? For a home office the company recognizes the issues of lower bandwidth and offers appropriate tools.
- Software to download: Netbriefings suggests RealPlayer or Windows Media Player and works with the end user to generate instructions. Netbriefings requests that the company do a systems check to make sure that it's ready for the Webcast.
- Customer service: Netbriefings sets up a customer service line so that end users can be a part of the program and to make sure that everyone has the best experience possible.

Netbriefings was frank about the other difficulties with Webcasts. Most of these issues lie within the internal network of a company and can be described as an internal bandwidth problem. After a consultation meeting, Netbriefings determines if there is enough bandwidth or if an outside server on the public Internet should be utilized. In addition, there are also firewall issues and Netbriefings does its best to work out the firewall issues when the client initially goes to open up the demo and participate in the system check. With respect to many of the issues mentioned, Netbriefings suggests that PR professionals be ready to work with IT departments. However, there are many times that PR people do not want to work with IT, and Netbriefings steps in to make it a smoother process. Moving forward, Anderson is certain that Webcasts will be the mode of communication of the future with increasing quality, ease of use, and more bandwidth for better quality connections.

JOURNALISTS ARE INTERESTED

Journalists we've talked to have mixed feeling about Webcasts. Many admit they'd much rather read the text of an executive's remarks than spend the time watching a speech live on a Webcast. On the other hand, there are big news events like corporate earnings reports or major product announcements that journalists want to see live as they happen so that stories can be written immediately.

The use of limited-access Webcasts by many companies to convey earnings information to investors was not well received by journalists and caused news organizations to press for access. Their pressure helped bring about Regulation FD in October 2000 from the SEC, which requires fair disclosure of events affecting public companies. Companies must now provide advance notification to concerned parties, including the media, that a disclosure is forthcoming, including details on how to participate in the event. Parties that are Webcasting can offer the notification through a news release or the company's Web site. (For more on what journalists think of Webcasts, see our interview with Bob Turner of *Video Systems* magazine on page 135 in this chapter.)

The bottom line for any PR person planning a Webcast is to focus on the quality of the audience member's experience. What's the point of having the most sophisticated technology or these incredibly dynamic online events incorporating visual PR if end users cannot fully enjoy the company's offering? It's really up to the PR professionals to work with all the parties involved in the Webcast to make sure that users are fully prepared to view the online events. It's really no different than the preparation for an offline event. PR professionals spend countless hours in preparation to make sure the audience members receive everything that they need prior to the event (i.e., invitations, company announcements, reminders, directions, etc.). It's also important to consider the content of the event. Having interesting content that is pertinent to the audience members to keep their attention is key.

Some of the most successful online events involve CEO announcements and keynote speeches, breaking company news, and investor relations information to attract the media, analysts, investors, and company stockholders. Keeping all of these considerations in mind and working with professionals that are skilled in online events moves the PR professional that much closer to understanding and being prepared to execute a successful online event. PR professionals can now take advantage of solid online public relations strategies to engage their brands beyond the normal day-to-day interactions of their audiences. The hype of the Webcast is over and the process has been demystified. We're now dealing with a huge communication tool that works in favor of the brand.

MEDIA INTERVIEW: BOB TURNER OF VIDEO SYSTEMS MAGAZINE

We spoke with Bob Turner, who has been writing about film and video editing issues for more than 20 years. For 14 of those years he was on the masthead of *Videography* magazine. More recently he's been a contributing editor for Primedia's *Video Systems* and editor of the company's electronic publication, "Bob Turner's THE CUT." His articles also appear in *Broadcast Engineering* and *Millimeter* magazine. Bob answered a series of questions regarding his use and interest in Webcasts.

1. Do you think Webcasts are an effective tool for journalists to receive information?

Turner: Yes, especially if Webcasts are available for pausing and replaying and time shifting. Too often, there is a schedule conflict that limits coverage. Also, this would need to be available only to journalists, or else there is little motivation for the journalists to write about what was said on the Webcast.

I have used Webcasts on several occasions on which to base articles and columns. Webcasts that include PowerPoints on one screen window and the speaker on another window are even better. If the bandwidth becomes a problem, at least I can understand what is being said with the PowerPoint.

2. How often do you participate in Webcasts?

Turner: Less than I would like. At one time, it was so effective that the trade shows made them less effective to encourage greater attendance. I am afraid that two to five years ago, when the technology was first allowing such techniques, more were using this communication method than they are today. It is ironic, since today, the technology makes it much easier and affordable to communicate this way. I participate in this method only two to five times a year this way, because there are so few opportunities remaining to do so. The year that MacWorld first moved to New York City from Boston I may have participated in Web-streamed press conferences over 25 times. And that is in addition to the 10 telephone teleconferences.

3. Discuss a recent Webcast and why you think the event was effective.

Turner: The best was that first MacWorld Conference in New York City. It broadcast on multiple streaming formats (unlike the QuickTime-only broadcasts afterwards that failed miserably because the single format could not handle the demand). The conference offered many interviews with hotlinks and separate windows with bullet points of speakers and links for additional information. The presentations were available for several days and could be paused and backed up to facilitate note taking after the live event. At this MacWorld, almost every vendor had a Web site link available on the MacWorld site. Alas, this is no longer the case, and MacWorld has made it necessary to actually attend if one wants to gain the information required.

I have also "attended" academic Web conferences with a speaker on the left window, graphics on the right frame, and indexes in the lower left that facilitated navigation after the live event was over. The graphics, mostly PowerPoint, assisted in keeping the focus on what was being communicated in spite of rather poor video. I have also participated in press announcements with well-edited components, which were clear and concise communications followed by talking head Q&A. This also proved quite effective.

4. Do you think journalists are logging on more often to Webcasts when they cannot physically attend an event?

Turner: I am afraid it depends on what can be expected from the Webcast. The technology now allows for an excellent communications experience, but frequently, the design of the Webcast has deteriorated to the point that it is frequently not worth the time.

Having said that, I believe that most journalists are doing most of their research, gaining documentation, and frequently "interviewing" over the Internet. Webcasts can be very effective, but it appears that they are actually effective far less than they used to be. The desire of journalists to gain that information is still there, but the willingness to use this technology effectively by the message providers appears to be less strong than it was in the recent past.

5. If you had a choice, would you rather attend an event or log online?

Turner: If all else were equal I would rather attend an online event.

6. In your experience, please discuss what you have found to be the pros and cons of Webcasts.

Turner: The pros of a Webcast are that it can be attended in a nonlinear way. I can stop and answer a telephone call, or back up the stream and repeat it or pause and take notes. Also, it can easily incorporate previously produced messages, and it can include graphics and text to complement the program. I can avoid the wasted time and expense of travel and time away from my family.

The cons include the possibility of being distracted by other events in my office environment. I might not find it as easy to gain specific answers or exclusive insights via the confidential question after the event. I would miss interacting with colleagues and sharing analysis. And of course there are the benefits attendant upon such events, including food and small gifts—plus the opportunity to escape from the office and place yourself in a new setting with some face-to-face social conversation and perhaps a chance to see friends and colleagues that you frequently do not get to spend time with. And you can focus on the communications presented without environmental pressures you might experience in your normal office setting.

Of course journalists can miss aspects of the communication without the ability to "rewind and replay" the event. Being taken away from other duties for travel can be stressful and expensive. And if you need to do more than a day trip, you may not sleep as well in a bed that is not your own. These all contribute to my conclusion that I would clearly prefer the far more efficient and effective Webcast communication, when such a Web-based event is done properly.

Finally, for the company with the message, if the location is a convention with many press conferences, the single message from a company can be lost by the many messages a journalist is bombarded with.

7. Do you find that archived Webcasts (or video on demand) are useful?

Turner: It may be one of the most useful aspects for me personally, as indicated by previous statements. Tie this with links for additional information, enough illustrations and photos to complement it, and even a transcript of the event to assist with accurate quotations, and it will be far more desirable for me to select that event as a basis for a column than a poorly created one. ■

PR Newswire is capturing the attention of many of its clients with the ability to provide Webcasting services through Thomson Financial. As experts in media distribution, PR Newswire gave us insight into this steadily growing business. We spoke with Michelle Savage, vice president of investor relations services, who immediately told us that "Webcasting is becoming a standard service and PR Newswire is working to demystify the process."

First and foremost, Savage explained, PR Newswire provides Webcasts for two reasons. From a regulatory standpoint, Webcasts can help protect against selective disclosure by ensuring that all interested parties have access to the same information at the same time. This makes company communications more "fair." The concept of fair disclosure is a driving force behind the investment community's use of Webcasts. Many PR Newswire clients are using their Webcasting services. "It's almost an insurance policy," stated Savage. "You can be on a telephone call with a select group of analysts, but through the Webcast you can inform the general public at the same time." PR Newswire is mandated to provide notification (although a specified time frame is not given). In accordance with Reg. FD, the company sends out a news release notice five days in advance and then the day of the Webcast (similar to a media advisory). All interested parties are notified, giving clients "peace of mind." The second major reason is for broader exposure. According to Savage and most of the professionals we've been dealing with, Webcasting is a great way to reach analysts who couldn't participate otherwise. The ability to reach more professionals in the investment community is one of the prime reasons why PR Newswire teamed up with Thomson Financial. Savage explained how Thomson added value to the Webcasting services. With a product called First Call, Thomson offers a database of sell-side analysts who make buy and sell recommendations on stocks and who need to be invited to the Webcasts affecting the companies they follow. The objective of Webcasting is not just posting an event—it's to deliver a message to a key audience. Two key audiences for PR Newswire's clients include the media and the investors. PR Newswire has the ability to successfully reach both target audiences.

Savage also commented on how more companies are using the service. These industries vary, encompassing everything from computers and high-tech to health care and pharmaceuticals. Of all the industries, computers and high-tech represent the highest percentage with respect to continued use of the services. However, within every industry there are preliminary considerations of which PR professionals need to be aware:

■ Where is the event going to take place?

■ Is it really going to reach the media?

■ What type of reporting is available after the event?

■ Is a registration report provided?

■ Can the company follow up with the Webcast participants?

■ Will all audiences have the ability to access the event (keeping in mind modem speed, firewall, and type of media player)?

■ Will the Webcast satisfy Reg. FD?

■ Is the reason for Webcasting cost efficient?

According to PR Newswire's company research, customers using the service are not only satisfied, but they also are repeat users. PR Newswire has seen a large increase in volume both with existing customers who continually use the Webcasting services and among new clients discovering how the company makes Web services simple and affordable. ■

PR INTERVIEW: MARK DeLAURENTIS OF MultiVu

Mark DeLaurentis, divisional vice president, Eventcasting for MultiVu, a PR Newswire company, shared his thoughts regarding the increase in Webcasting. He started with PR Newswire in April 1999 and saw how the use of video in Webcasting peaked and then died off when the economy went into a recession in 2001. There was much more of a need for audio and teleconference Web services. However, as of 2002, video in Webcasts is on the rise. This fluctuation could be attributed to the fact that there is a price differential between audio and video Webcasting. Audio services cost anywhere from $700 to $4,000. Video, on the other hand, can include a full broadcast production, which can start at $15,000.

Regardless of audio or video, Webcasts have captured the attention of the media. DeLaurentis gave the example of the Republican Party's National Convention Webcast launching the party's convention Web site months prior to the convention and ensuing campaign. Some of the most well-known journalists logged on to the Web site, and the result was excellent print coverage. It also drew the attention of major journalists who cover Capitol Hill for television and radio. Another good example of a Webcast that attracted key journalists is that of Sabre Systems. DeLaurentis stated that this reservations company needed a Webcast in 90 minutes and PR Newswire was able to furnish the request. Although the time frame was short, the Webcast attracted key media including *The Wall Street Journal* and major daily newspapers.

"It's the new direction of Webcasts," he said, referring to the compressed production time. "The future of Webcasting is an always-on scenario," he added. "It's the ability to have the Webcast quickly and efficiently. The day has arrived when a CEO can walk out of the office and right into a studio to communicate to investors or employees through Webcasting," he continued. What makes a company such as PR Newswire and its clients move closer toward this "always-on" scenario is the greater need for Webcasting services, and the recognition in the market that a well-designed program by a qualified company can deliver a strong message. DeLaurentis said that when PR Newswire contemplates a Webcast it does an extensive amount of consulting. One of the first questions answered is this: Should the Webcast be an audio Webcast with a synched PowerPoint presentation or should it be a video Webcast? Audio Webcasts are popular and can include a presenter-controlled slide presentation. By using slides and graphics, companies can appeal to a visual society. DeLaurentis advised that without the slides and graphics, audience retention declines.

However, in the case of earnings, this is a distinct group of listeners who do not necessarily need an accompanying slide presentation. DeLaurentis recommends a video when the content of the Webcast warrants one. Examples include panel discussions, or when the CEO of the company wants to present visually to a group. Of course, video is more expensive. A MultiVu "Automated Audiocast" takes advantage of existing technology and allows for communicators to present from their office with a slide show directly to their virtual audience on the Web. These Webcasts can be too long and might lose the attention of audiences. Succinct messaging through Webcasting can be incredibly powerful because companies can reach their target audiences as easily as distributing or e-mailing the link. Even the major launch of a product only requires a half-hour presentation and then time for Q&A. Almost all videocast models are based on one hour. The time issue does not apply to all situations but it is something serious to consider.

DeLaurentis ended the interview with a focus on the future of the Webcast. He discussed how robotic cameras will continue to make inroads in video production, as will compressed production schedules with rapid turnaround. "Getting crucial information to your target audiences rapidly is what Webcasting is all about. At MultiVu we continue to develop our services that break down the barriers of reaching the customers and investors that buy company products and invest in company stock. This powerful new medium has yet to reach its potential and as broadband continues to grow, the desire for content will only increase." ■

PR INTERVIEW:
PAT MEIER OF PAT MEIER ASSOCIATES

Pat Meier is a broadcast journalist by training, as is her husband, who has also worked as a cinematographer. She describes their interest in Webcasts as "a natural merger" that has brought together a PR firm and a Webcast company, 1Webcast (*1webcast.com*).

"There are certainly things you can say verbally—be it audio or video—that you simply can't say in print," says Meier, explaining the importance of a smile, a wink, or another facial expression in indicating whether a speaker is being sarcastic, facetious, or dead serious. Video can also be important in conveying whether the CEO or other top executives have "passion" for what they're doing or are simply working for a paycheck, she says.

Meier, whose Mill Valley, California, firm represents many technology companies, favors preproduced video segments of five or six minutes over live, event-driven Webcasts. The latter are needed, she says, in the case of quarterly earnings reports, but can generally be handled with audio-only services provided by a number of vendors. Packaged video segments, by contrast, put the power of the producer in the hands of the client and the PR people and enable them to craft the message and the accompanying images in ways not possible when your client accepts an invitation to be on CNBC or a radio show. "By Webcasting, you actually are your own medium," she says.

Webcasting lets you go around CNBC or other media outlets to reach your client's customers directly, she says. Journalists will also find value in the Webcasts if they are done in a proper tone without being sales-oriented, she says. "You can't be so hypey or airy-fairy that it's a puff piece."

Meier says Webcasts are their own tool and therefore don't need to fit into your traditional practices. You might not ordinarily issue a press release to have your CEO comment on a competitor's product announcement, she says, but it's okay to put a Webcast online in which the CEO comments on competitors' announcements and other industry events. "You can do your own roundtable and become your own experts," she says. She recommends a quick e-mail to select groups of journalists to alert them when such Webcasts are put online.

Video production equipment is less expensive than it used to be, Meier says, and does not require an elaborate studio. Meier's firm orchestrates independent press lunches during major computer trade shows, such as Comdex, CES, and Siggraph, and has made a small business out of creating brief video Webcasts for the companies that sponsor or showcase at the press luncheons. As part of the sponsorship fee, Meier's firm will shoot the video in the restaurant, do the editing in a hotel room, and post the video on Meier's Web site (*patmeier.com*), where it can be linked to by any of the sponsoring companies.

Meier says an executive who is willing to devote time to appearing on a supposedly news-oriented Web site with questionable claims of audience size should instead be persuaded to invest his or her time and a little money in hiring a film or video crew to create a Webcast that the company controls. Young producers are out there, she says, but you want one who will produce a mainstream Webcast rather than something avant garde, or, worse yet, too salesy for use by legitimate news organizations. "You don't want to be glitzy," she cautions, but she does recommend at least a little makeup to keep your CEO from looking shiny and untrustworthy.

Another important ingredient to feature in a Webcast is your client's customers, Meier notes. Getting people to talk about how your client's product or service has brought change for the better to their organization can be very powerful in attracting media coverage or in winning over prospective customers who might be visiting the client's Web site. "There has to be a delta," Meier says. "How were things before? How are they now?"

One thing to remember as you move forward with Webcasts is not to forget about reporters who might still be accessing the Internet over a 56K modem, Meier says. She recommends identifying the best few seconds of a four-minute Webcast and offering that as "an excerpt" to reporters. Your e-mail that alerts them to the Webcast should provide one URL for the full Webcast and another for the excerpt, or one encoded for low-bandwidth connections and one for higher speeds. "It's also nice to back up an interview with a transcript," she notes. ■

III PROTECTING THE BRAND

10. MONITORING BRAND COMMUNICATION

> Knowing what is said about your online client is as important as knowing what's said in print.
> Vendors offer affordable search services that are more efficient than doing it on your own.
> Think carefully before responding to postings or trying to manipulate a discussion group with messages that favor your client.

The earlier chapters of this book should have left you with an improved sense of how the Internet can help you get the message out about your clients and their brands. Smarter use of e-mail, newsletters, and Webcasts is going to help you reach more reporters and consumers than was possible in the old, offline world. However, we've also noted that this new environment bears close watching because it is a forum that never sleeps—a network that can sprout a new message board, chat room, or a Web site at any hour of any day—and people can use these forums to praise or attack your client and its brands. Ignoring this arena could mean getting a late start in fighting a false statement or rumor after it has had time to gain credence among potential customers.

In Chapter 4, we suggested that you become familiar with monitoring services like eWatch of PR Newswire so you could find out which reporters are covering what topics. In this chapter, we aim to make a strong case for working with a monitoring company to get as complete a picture as possible of what is being said about your clients online by reporters and by the general public.

Several large PR firms offer their own monitoring services, promising to keep their clients aware on a daily or hourly basis of important references to their companies and brands in online newspapers, newsletters, Web sites, and discussion groups. Many of the firms get their data from vendors such as eWatch, Burrelle's, and CyberAlert, which also work directly with clients eager to keep up with online postings about their companies and brands.

The services have created search engines that can be fed the keywords most likely to be associated with your client. The search software is then unleashed across the Internet to uncover all examples of news stories, message board postings, or chat room comments that might relate to your client. The services are not foolproof. They cannot report on chat room comments if they are not archived in some fashion. Some do not search subscription-based Web sites such as *The Wall Street Journal*'s. None of them will find online references to your company on Web sites that do not use the Roman alphabet, because their search engines generally do not handle Japanese, Chinese, Greek, or Cyrillic characters.

Despite their failings, many PR people who subscribe to monitoring services are extremely enthusiastic about their value. "I think every brand in every company should be monitoring online," says David Dunne, executive vice president and director of operations for Edelman Interactive Solutions. His agency offers a Web monitoring service called I-Wire that is based on data retrieved by eWatch. "Every time we monitor for a brand or a company we are pleasantly surprised by the depth of data we can produce," says Dunne, who has done monitoring for many clients, including Apple Computer and Microsoft's Xbox game player.

A major reason why Apple has offered its iMac computer in so many colors is the feedback received by monitoring online discussion groups, says Dunne. Apple has a loyal customer base that participates in online groups and was quite vocal in requesting more color choices, he says. Another Edelman client, Dunne says, discovered bugs in its software products through Web monitoring and ended up having its engineers participate in the groups to make customers aware of patches that were available and to recruit some newsgroup participants for the company's own beta testers' group for future releases. (For more on Dunne's experiences with Web monitoring, see our interview with him on page 160 in this chapter.)

Bill Comcowich, CEO of Connecticut-based CyberAlert Inc., says the value of Web monitoring is not yet apparent to many PR people who remain preoccupied with counting how many of their press releases are picked up in a limited number of prominent print publications. He says clients are concerned about the reputation of their brands in all media, not just the major newspapers and magazines, and companies like CyberAlert are well positioned to report on how a company and its brands are being discussed. "There's clearly a movement to measure the value of PR or the return on investment [ROI]," he says. "This kind of technology is going to be crucial in that movement toward ROI."

One way in which CyberAlert can be most valuable, Comcowich says, is in helping clients respond immediately to attacks on themselves or their brands. Many companies have found themselves to be the subject of derogatory Web sites with names like *chasesucks.com*, which are established primarily to post negative comments about a company and its goods or services. Services like CyberAlert's give customers the ability to get regular reports on postings to such Web sites without having to tap one of their own people to monitor the site. At the same time, the customer gets reports on postings—both negative and positive—that occur on thousands of other Web sites and newsgroups. In fact, many companies find out about positive things their far-flung companies are doing in the way of corporate philanthropy and community goodwill, of which they might otherwise not be aware.

Comcowich says companies do not need to respond to every negative remark made on an Internet message board, but he believes in the value of responding quickly to misinformation that shows signs of spreading quickly to other forums and possibly into the mainstream press. CyberAlert's customers generally consider their use of the service to be a trade secret, so Comcowich isn't able to name them. However, he does talk about how CyberAlert helped a chemical company become aware that it was a target of a protest movement taking shape online against genetically modified foods. The company used this information to defend itself by shaping the debate on its terms. Similarly, CyberAlert says it helped a software company become aware of a bug in one of its programs that was angering consumers. A credit card company, meanwhile, found out that consumers were complaining online about a delay in the posting of payments and it traced the problem to a business partner that it subsequently replaced. An insurance company, meanwhile, said it found out that independent brokers were misrepresenting the benefits of the company's policies. A drug company found out that doctors were prescribing one of its medicines inappropriately.

When we spoke to CyberAlert in 2002 its customers were paying a flat rate of $395 a month with no additional costs per clipping or for additional keywords. Comcowich would not divulge the size of his client base, but he did say that his company was handling 2,000 searches a day. CyberAlert was delivering clips daily, but it was planning to offer more frequent reporting on more limited numbers of Web sites.

PR people who might not have the budget for such a monitoring service might find support among other executives at their company who are charged with strategic planning. One way Web monitoring services have proven effective has been in monitoring the activities of competitors to discover their product plans and other initiatives—sometimes before they are officially announced. Sometimes a new initiative can be revealed in a Web page mistakenly put online too early or in online listings of new positions that indicate a competitor is ramping up in some particular area.

Comcowich set up a guest account for us so we could judge the value of CyberAlert for ourselves. He provided us with a login we could use at the *cyberalert.com* site to monitor searches he created for us. We also received daily e-mails containing the latest results for ongoing searches. A search for Krispy Kreme, a rapidly expanding North Carolina-based doughnut maker, turned up dozens of hits during our demonstration period and pointed out the wide variety of ways in which brand names are invoked on the Internet.

In one day, Krispy Kreme earned a mention in *The Honolulu Star-Bulletin* in a business trend story as an example of a company that had changed the ticker symbol on its stock. An announcement of Krispy Kreme's intention to expand into new markets was reported in a number of publications from El Paso, Texas, to Amarillo, Texas, to Billings, Montana, to North Carolina. However, CyberAlert's results also would have provided a PR person with some examples of the negative consequences of being a fast-growing brand. In one example, the company's fantastic success in Minnesota was used against it by two different letter writers in *The Star Tribune*. One lamented that Minnesotans were more likely to support Krispy Kreme than the Twins baseball team and the other noted that one town had spent a half-million dollars on doughnuts in one week even though it was unwilling to invest in school improvements. In another example, the *State Journal-Register* of Springfield, Illinois, reported some anti-Krispy Kreme sentiment in noting the choice of Midwest rival Mel-O-Cream for a local school fund-raiser rather than using an "out-of-town business."

Krispy Kreme's PR representatives might also be interested in how Krispy Kreme has worked its way into the vernacular of Internet bulletin board posters. Whereas one was raising a Krispy Kreme donut in a toast to a fellow newsgroup participant, another was professing his "hate" for the donuts in a newsgroup devoted to Disney theme parks. Teen site gURL.com, meanwhile, invoked the company's name in a way sure to be unpopular with doughnut marketers, suggesting that boy bands "are pumped out like so many overglazed Krispy Kreme donuts."

Nancy Sells of eWatch, a Minnesota-based unit of PR Newswire, says she continues to be surprised by how many PR people are not yet looking on the Internet for references—both positive and negative—to their clients and their brands. Sells says she still sees big stacks of paper clippings when she visits prospective clients. "There's something about visual presentation that's still important," she says.

The challenge for eWatch, she says, is to persuade PR people that they need to go beyond paper clippings to keep up with the Internet forums that are shaping public opinion. So much of what appears on the Internet will never appear on paper, she notes, pointing to not only bulletin boards, but to so much of the extra content that newspapers and magazines place on their Web sites that does not make it into print. "Many of them don't understand that what is available online might never appear anywhere else," she says of PR practitioners. "It's up to us to articulate our value."

The recession that followed the dot-com bust has only made it more difficult to get people to examine new services, says Sells. When we spoke to eWatch in 2002 it was selling five different services—covering Web publications, investor boards, newsgroups, online forums, and Web sites—each for $3,900 a year. A customer who subscribed to all five was paying $17,500 a year.

We put eWatch to work tracking references to Krispy Kreme's competitor Dunkin' Donuts and were again impressed with the results. Like CyberAlert, eWatch returned a large number of references from all across the Internet. The company's PR people would certainly be interested in the various stories reporting on the planned opening of new franchises from Oconee County, Georgia, to West Chicago, Illinois. One newsgroup participant was critical of Dunkin' Donuts for not offering a store locator on its Web site—an erroneous claim that might be worth correcting. An article on Billboard's *billboard.com*, meanwhile, showed the value of attaching your corporate name to a sports arena as the Dunkin' Donuts Center in Providence, Rhode Island, was listed as a venue for the Rock Fest concert tour. An Associated Press story, however, reflected the downside of such associations as the Dunkin' Donuts name was linked to a report on the indictment of the arena's acting executive director on theft charges.

eWatch's results also indicated the extent to which Dunkin' Donuts is part of American culture, for both positive and negative reasons. One newspaper story reported on a Massachusetts bank robber who asked that the teller fill his Dunkin' Donuts bag with cash while he calmly ate a doughnut. A report in *The Providence Journal* noted that the corruption trial of that city's mayor had featured an audiotape made by the FBI of conversations in a local Dunkin' Donuts store. Various newsgroups featured contributors who were sipping Dunkin' Donuts coffee as they sat at their keyboards and some were concerned about traffic patterns around their local Dunkin' Donuts store. A Web pub called "The Straits Times" noted in a career advice article that singer Madonna had a rough start as a Dunkin' Donuts clerk who was fired for squirting jam at a customer. Perhaps more useful to a PR person, though, was a mention in *The New Haven Register* of a breast cancer walkathon that featured free doughnuts donated by the Campbell Avenue franchise in West Haven, Connecticut.

A third player in the Web monitoring game is Burrelle's Information Services, the 114-year veteran of the paper-clipping business. In the last 10 years it has moved steadily toward the electronic realm, offering monitoring of publication Web sites, newsgroups, and other forums. Given the large base of customers it has for paper clippings, Burrelle's might be in the best position to move many of its customers to Web monitoring, whereas its competitors like CyberAlert and eWatch must first identify those prospective customers, establish relationships with them, and persuade them that Web monitoring is a new service that they need.

Even so, it hasn't been an easy sell, according to Bruce Merchant, executive vice president of Burrelle's. "There's a need to do an educational process with many clients," he says. "What they really value is still the traditional press," he adds. "There's a large part of our client base who still wants to smell ink and get ink on their fingers."

Merchant says many PR professionals cite two common arguments against Web monitoring. "The perception is that everything on the Web is free so why would I pay Burrelle's to monitor the Web?" he says. Another frequently heard comment is "I'm not ready to jump into that pond just yet."

In response, Merchant argues that Internet content is important because what is said online can really hurt a company. He points, as an example, to a downturn in Berkshire Hathaway's stock in recent years that was linked to message board comments about the supposedly failing health of chairman Warren Buffett.

Companies that think they can handle the monitoring on their own are in for a rude awakening, Merchant says, noting that Burrelle's has refined its search procedures over the years and still comes up with a lot of garbage of little value to its clients. "Eighty percent of what we find on the Internet is discarded," he says, noting the importance that Burrelle's places on employing human editors who review search results and share only the most relevant ones with clients.

This human intervention, however, comes at a price. When we spoke to Merchant in 2002, a client who wanted immediate electronic notification of relevant newsgroup postings or Web references was being charged $175 a month for Burrelle's NewsAlert service plus $3.71 for every clip that an editor found to be consistent with the client's interests. Burrelle's was also printing out newsgroup and Web references and mailing them to clients as part of a service that cost $287 a month plus $1.58 per clipping.

Merchant acknowledges that Burrelle's could operate more efficiently if it were possible to electronically retrieve all pertinent references to a client regardless of source—print, Web, newsgroup—and share them electronically with clients. He says that day is coming within several years, but a major barrier that must still be overcome is copyright restrictions that keep Burrelle's from making electronic copies of articles to share with clients. The company subscribes to paper publications so it can cut out articles for its clients, but many newspaper and magazine publishers are seeking to make money on their own electronic archives and have not yet been willing to discuss arrangements with Burrelle's that would enable the clipping company to deliver articles electronically. "From a publisher's point of view, it's not on the radar screen," he says.

REPORTERS ARE ALREADY THERE

If postings by individuals are not enough of a concern for you or your client, then consider the fact that reporters are also online trolling for information and opinions that might find their way into articles—thereby gaining immediate credibility. Reporters we know say they frequently search newsgroups and Web sites for information about companies and brands they're assigned to cover. It can take a lot of digging in search of elusive gems, but journalists say it can be worth the effort when they find a newsgroup contributor who is a current employee, former employee, business partner, or otherwise knowledgeable source about a company or its products. Sometimes, an individual post can be a story by itself, as in the case of the flaw in Intel's Pentium computer chip that came to the attention of reporters in 1994 after an e-mail discussion started by a Virginia math professor ended up in a CompuServe discussion forum. We're also reminded of the negative press about Lexis-Nexis in 1996 that was fed by message board postings by people angry about a new research service that revealed the Social Security numbers of private citizens.

More recently, *The New York Times* reported in its July 15, 2002 edition that the troubles facing *The Adventures of Pluto Nash*, an Eddie Murphy movie from Warner Brothers and Castle Rock Entertainment, could be tied to an Internet posting. *The Times* said that negative publicity preceding the movie's release could be traced to a five-paragraph negative review posted on a Web site called Ain't It Cool News (*aintitcoolnews.com*) by someone who had attended a preview screening in Pasadena, California. A reference to the review by *Time* magazine helped spread the negative news and got more people associating *Pluto Nash* with words like "flop" and "turkey" before it even hit theaters.

Wendy M. Grossman, a freelance writer and book author who has written for *Scientific American*, *New Scientist*, and *The Daily Telegraph* from her post in the United Kingdom, says newsgroups are usually most useful in making reporters aware of potential sources who can be interviewed privately offline. Files of frequently asked questions (FAQs) are also very useful in educating reporters about topics that might be new to them. Bombshell posts like the one about the Pentium flaw are pretty rare. Nevertheless, Grossman says her own recreational reading of the rec.sport.tennis newsgroup resulted in a book review for *Tennis Magazine* when a posting made her aware of a new book by Nathalie Tauziat, a French player, that was being released only in France. In another case, she developed articles for *Scientific American* and *The Daily Telegraph* about the potential disaster of the Y2K computer problem after reading the comp.software.year-2000 newsgroup. (Read more about Grossman's use of newsgroups in our interview with her on page 163 in this chapter.)

What to Do With the Information

The chief complaint among customers of Web monitoring services seems to be a feeling of being flooded with information and an inability to know what to do with it. The e-mail reports generated by a CyberAlert or an eWatch should probably be directed at a staff member who has some time to review them regularly to decide what, if anything, needs to be addressed. Those clippings about how your company has sponsored the annual walk for breast cancer can probably be filed for the next time you want to publicize your public service. Any newsgroup posting that reveals a reporter seeking help with a story can be addressed easily enough with an e-mail to the reporter in which you offer to be of assistance. (Most times, however, reporters will probably monitor groups passively and not announce their participation with a posting.) Similarly, the PR person for Krispy Kreme would be within his or her rights to contact gURL.com to remind the site's operators that Krispy Kreme sells a variety of different doughnuts.

What should be done with the postings in which an anonymous person with a bizarre and often vulgar pseudonym is making awful and false statements about the mental capacity of your CEO? In most cases we'd urge caution before engaging those who post comments online in discussions. Corporate representatives are often not well received in many newsgroups where participants are made uncomfortable and sometimes hostile by the feeling that they are being watched. People are entitled to their right to free speech, after all, and much of what is uttered in discussion groups amounts to opinion. In the rare cases in which you believe a posting is a deliberate distortion intended to deflate the company's stock or otherwise injure its reputation, we suggest talking to your attorney about how to proceed. Public companies need to be particularly careful because SEC disclosure regulations require companies to publicize whatever they might divulge in an Internet discussion group, which means that your response might get more attention than the original Internet posting and give instant legitimacy to the topic that a critic has raised.

What is true of negative newsgroup postings is also true of negative Web sites of the *chasesucks.com* variety. Any kind of "cease and desist" message you send is likely to be posted to the site as a rallying cry for more public support. A better tactic might be to review the site for evidence of why it was founded. Did the founder have a particular negative experience with your company? Is there anything your company can offer the founder as fair compensation for that experience? A quiet resolution will probably serve your company better than an antagonistic approach that all but guarantees press attention and more traffic to the Web site in question.

If you decide that the damage caused by a Web site owner or message board poster far outweighs the cost of a legal battle, there are ways to track down the offenders. The Whois database of domain names is administered by Network Solutions and accessible through *networksolutions.com*. It will provide you with the name and contact information that was provided when a domain name was paid for. A check of that database reveals, for example, that the infamous *chasesucks.com* domain is now in the hands of Chase Manhattan Bank. Other companies, such as the Internet Crimes Group Inc. of Princeton, New Jersey, can assist you in identifying the real names of message board contributors who often hide behind fictitious screen names.

MANIPULATING MESSAGE BOARDS

If message boards are powerful forums for affecting how people think about a company or its brands, then you are probably wondering how you might use them proactively—rather than reactively in response to criticisms or attacks. Not surprisingly, some smart colleagues in public relations have already gone down this road with some success. Among them is Helen Donlon of Arts PR & Publicity International, a book publicist in Great Britain, who has been sure to communicate with newsgroups devoted to music stars prior to the publication of books about those stars. "I would highly recommend it to anyone," says Donlon, who has used newsgroups to promote books about Bob Dylan, Tom Jones, ABBA, and Queen.

Donlon says she is always wary of intruding on the newsgroup's discussion so she typically begins her postings by typing "for anyone interested . . . " and always includes her e-mail address so people can follow up with her outside the newsgroup. She says she offered early review copies of books to newsgroup contributors and succeeded in getting some well-written reviews that were ready for distribution on the day the book was published. "We got a commendation for our ABBA biography from a 'leading fan' who is the well-respected (in the ABBA community) host of an Australian Weblist," Donlon wrote in an e-mail interview. "His commendation for our book was priceless. Fans are often the harshest critics about books on their heroes after all, so getting his seal of approval was vital!"

Several marketing agencies in the United States have also recognized the potential in promoting positive mentions of a client in online forums and are offering a service known as "newsgroup seeding." Among the practitioners is Liquid Advertising, based in Pacific Palisades, California, which offers the service among its menu of "online covert operations."

CEO Will Akerlof says Liquid Advertising employs college interns to generate buzz in newsgroups primarily on behalf of clients in the entertainment industry like FX Networks, Universal Studios, and Fandango. "You have to hire people who are intelligent and know how to use newsgroups well," he says.

Akerlof says Liquid Advertising will identify which newsgroups are of interest to the target audience for a movie or TV show and its interns will then post to those groups using the lingo that is appropriate. He notes, for example, that interns might try to promote a movie like *The Fast and the Furious* in newsgroups related to street racing. "They really have to be fluent in the patois of what's being discussed."

Aware of the possible negative reaction to commercially driven comments, the interns usually do not identify themselves as Liquid Advertising employees, he says. Frequently they will say they are college students who are working on a project, he says, and their requests for information are generally well received by other newsgroup participants. "It's a very inexpensive way to get quite a lot of market research very quickly," he says.

Posts to newsgroups should be short, he says. "I think you'd get a lot more people upset by posting press releases," he says.

Akerlof says newsgroup seeding might not be appropriate for all kinds of products or services. "No one really wants to discuss their favorite laundry detergent or toothpaste," he says. Other highly specialized newsgroups related to a particular car model, for example, are more likely to recognize a commercially motivated message and respond in a hostile way to the company or product being promoted.

Another drawback for seeding, he says, is the difficulty of calculating the return on the investment. The newsgroup messages are meant to generate buzz and not inspire the immediate sale of something on an e-commerce site, he notes. Liquid Advertising has had some success in counting page views of a particular URL that it has promoted in newsgroup postings, but long, trackable unique URLs like those used in many e-mail newsletters are not appropriate in a newsgroup posting that is supposed to appear informal and without commercial motive.

Nevertheless, Akerlof predicts greater usage of newsgroup seeding in those areas where buzz is deemed important. One such area might be the political arena, he says, noting the benefits that might be achieved by a political campaign that makes sure participants in a newsgroup devoted to environmental concerns or gun control are aware of a candidate's views on those topics.

Entertainment companies will also continue to use the tool, he says, explaining how dozens of newsgroups can be identified as places to promote every new movie based on the actors involved, the director, the artists on the soundtrack, and the subject matter of the movie.

As veteran users of the Internet, we should interject here that we see newsgroup seeding as a potentially troubling way to promote your client's interests. Newsgroups historically have been the region of the Internet with the strongest aversion to commercial messages, so there is great danger of exposing your client to a nasty backlash. Making full disclosure of who you are and who you represent makes the most sense to us, as it protects you from having that fact discovered at some point during the discussion to discredit you or criticize your client. It is probably true that entertainment-related fan sites used by Donlon and Liquid Advertising are most accepting of marketing messages and good results like the book reviews solicited by Donlon can be achieved. However, be careful to do your homework and to test the water before diving in.

In our next chapter, we talk about how your strategies for helping your clients cope with emergencies should include use of the Internet.

PR INTERVIEW: DAVID DUNNE OF EDELMAN'S INTERACTIVE SOLUTIONS

David Dunne is puzzled by the relatively small size of the Web monitoring business. He has an interest in promoting it because he is executive vice president and director of operations for Edelman Interactive Solutions, which includes the agency's I-Wire Internet monitoring service. However, Dunne is just befuddled by the overall lack of interest in monitoring services, whether they're offered by Edelman, CyberAlert, eWatch, or anyone else.

"It's just as important that people are monitoring online as it is offline," says Dunne, noting that PR people have always seen value in collecting clippings of newspapers and other publications. Listening to what is said online can provide PR people and their clients with "early warning" of problems with their products or services. "It's a great vehicle for getting that kind of feedback," he says.

"The Internet is the only place where people are interacting and speaking to each other," he adds. "It's an instant barometer of how people are feeling."

Anyone who questions the power of the Internet to cause problems for them or their brands should investigate the tremendous online success of Greenpeace, Dunne says. He notes that the group has closed many of its physical offices because it has used the Internet so effectively to get its messages out and to wage campaigns against companies that it believes are hurting the environment. "Greenpeace and other NGOs [nongovernmental organizations] earned a place at the table and companies know they can't ignore them," Dunne says.

Dunne says that many clients seem to be interested in online monitoring after a crisis has begun and they want to know how well their company or brand is recovering. Frequently, they will suspend the online monitoring until the next crisis arises, never realizing that consistent monitoring might help them avoid crises in the first place. "If companies are in the marketplace, they really have a responsibility to themselves and their stakeholders to know what people are saying about their brands," Dunne says.

"Every time we monitor for a brand or a company we are pleasantly surprised by the depth of the data we can produce," Dunne says, noting particular successes in monitoring for Apple Computer Inc. He recalls how the introduction of the iMac sparked a lot of discussion in Apple-related discussion groups about the initial limited choice of color options. "We found enormous brand vibrations in that chatter," he recalls, noting that some discussion participants were recruited to advise Apple on future product development.

Dunne says he generally recommends monitoring discussions passively to keep track of what is being said, but Edelman has occasionally urged clients to become involved in the discussion. In one case, he says, engineers at a software company entered a discussion group and communicated with customers about a patch that they had developed for a bug in their company's software. In the odd case in which the client prefers that Edelman post to a newsgroup, Dunne says, the PR representatives are very careful to identify themselves. "We have nothing to gain by being cute and everything to lose," he says.

If a contributor to a discussion group is unfairly attacking the actions of a company, Edelman might advise the company to respond with a brief, simple message like "For the real facts, click here." That message should be linked to a Web page where the company can refute the criticisms in greater detail, he says.

Being up front and transparent is essential, Dunne says, if the PR industry is to avoid feeling the backlash from a public that will ultimately realize that some PR people are secretly influencing online discussion in favor of their clients. "The people who are engaged in that give the entire industry a bad reputation," he says.

Dunne acknowledges that the flow of information from monitoring vendors like eWatch can be heavy, but he urges companies to maintain their monitoring efforts even in difficult economic times. Having a long-term relationship with a monitoring service allows a company to refine the keywords it uses so that the results are closely on target with what the company seeks. Full-time monitoring also enables companies to become aware of postings before they spark PR crises. With costs of about $1,000 a month for some services, "that's a lease payment on a car for an executive," he says. An analysis service like Edelman's costs more, but the return on that investment can be "potentially priceless," he says, noting that clients receive insights that enable them to react early to changes in the market. ∎

MEDIA INTERVIEW:
WENDY M. GROSSMAN, FREELANCE WRITER

Wendy M. Grossman is a veteran journalist and Internet user who has written two books about the worldwide network, net.wars (NYU Press, 1998) and From Anarchy to Power: The Net Comes of Age (NYU Press, 2001). It is safe to say that she probably knows more about newsgroups and other online discussion forums than most other practicing reporters. Her advice to PR people is to stay tuned to what's happening in these online meeting places.

Grossman recalls writing a review of a book by French tennis player Nathalie Tauziat for Tennis Magazine because she found out about the book's forthcoming release through a posting on the rec.sport.tennis newsgroup. "At the time no one knew about it and I wouldn't have heard about it otherwise," Grossman notes. Having early knowledge was important, she says, because the book ultimately came out only in French and around the time of the French Open and Tauziat did not want to be distracted from her game. "It's all in my book," she told other reporters. "Read my book."

Another Usenet newsgroup called comp.software.year-2000 helped Grossman in her reporting on the pending disaster that was forecast due to the inability of critically important computer systems to correctly distinguish between 1900 and 2000. Her articles were published in Scientific American and The Daily Telegraph.

Despite such successes, Grossman does not advise reporters to slog through countless newsgroups in hopes of finding stories just waiting to be written. Instead, she says, newsgroups can be a good way to become educated about unfamiliar topics about which they hope to write. "My recommendation would be that you pick a couple of relevant newsgroups and skim through the last few weeks of postings," she says, noting for example, that fan newsgroups are particularly useful libraries of information for celebrity profiles. "Doing that should give you a feel for who the group's regulars are, and then you can e-mail them privately. You can, of course, post to the newsgroup, but you will get better responses if you can show that you've done your homework already—i.e., read some of the newsgroup, understand what topics it covers, etc."

Grossman also urges reporters and PR people interested in newsgroups to review the FAQs if the group maintains such a file. "If you're trying to come to grips with an unfamiliar technology—fishkeeping, how to take apart and clean your VCR, crypto—often those FAQs are an excellent introduction," she says. "If you do use a newsgroup for research, you should always read the FAQ before you start asking questions—it's rude to ask the regulars to explain stuff they've already explained thousands of times, and it makes you look like you're too stupid to talk to."

PR people who are willing to plow through a lot of useless postings are likely to come up with "a feel for what people and customers are thinking about your company," Grossman notes, but she urges caution before engaging in the online discussion. "No one can stop you from reading and saying nothing," she says. "But if you start posting, the temptation may be to pretend that you have no connection and you're a disinterested third party. Resist this temptation. State up front who you are and what you do. You will get some flak from people who see you as a handy target—but people on Usenet tend to see very quickly through PR efforts masquerading as genuine vox pop, and if you try to go that route you will be despised."

A PR person who is honest with the newsgroup and still receives a small number of negative comments should not be discouraged, Grossman says. "Once you become a familiar face, the vitriol will mostly pass." ■

11 NEW TOOLS FOR CRISIS MANAGEMENT

➤ PR professionals recognize the value of the Internet in a crisis situation.

➤ The Internet allows leaders to be direct and the public to be well informed.

➤ The Internet enables companies to respond quickly to negative publicity.

➤ Crisis Web sites should be developed before a crisis occurs.

As communicators, you've always concentrated on disseminating timely and credible information to inform the public, mold perceptions, and build stronger images for your companies or clients. The use of the Internet has helped enormously to build relationships, increase the frequency of communication, and enhance the targeted reach to those who need to hear a company's message. The earlier chapters of this book were meant to instruct and inform on the many strategies that are being employed to imsprove communications via the Internet during "normal" times or what's considered the scope of usual business activities. However, one area that we have not touched on is the uncertainty of communication when a crisis strikes and how imperative it is to act within a short time frame.

Many communicators agree that there's only a 12-hour window to influence press coverage and public opinion when tragedy or crisis strikes. Our definition of crisis is fairly broad, encompassing any event that promises to have a significant negative impact on your company or client—ranging from the discovery of accounting errors in financial statements to a CEO's indictment to a large tragedy on the scale of a plane crash or the terrorist attacks of September 11, 2001. In each of those cases, customers, employees, and stockholders look to the companies involved for answers, evidence of leadership, and a sign that there is a plan for getting back to "business as usual."

In decades past, it was commonly thought that crisis management plans were only needed in certain industries, such as transportation or manufacturing, where accidents were most likely to occur. However, a long list of factors—including everything from product tampering to product recalls to financial shenanigans to workplace violence—has changed all that. No business can feel totally secure that it will not be inundated tomorrow with inquiries from the media and the public about some event or accusation affecting its company, industry, or geographic area. Plans for managing these crises need to be based around the need to get information out quickly to your employees, their families, your customers, your stockholders, and the news media.

By this point in the book, it should not be too surprising that we think the Internet is an extremely important weapon in your crisis management arsenal. In the same way that the Internet deserves close attention for its ability to spread negative information like wildfire, it can be used to spread positive information quickly about how your company is handling a given crisis. E-mailed press releases can reach large numbers of reporters in a fraction of the time it would take to make phone calls or fax out releases. Web sites, meanwhile, can be built in advance of a crisis and "turned on" quickly to educate reporters, employees, stockholders, and others about the company and the steps it is taking to respond to events.

Building your crisis management strategy around the Internet makes sense for many reasons, including these:

- The decentralized nature of the network pretty much guarantees it will function even in times of tragedy when telephone systems might be inaccessible due to tremendous demand in the local area.

- The accessibility of the Internet makes it the perfect place for posting a clear statement of the company's communications objectives for senior executives and other employees who must stay focused on the message in difficult times.

- The Internet offers the ability to communicate directly to employees, customers, and stockholders in a timely fashion with up-to-the-minute updates if necessary.

- The Internet provides the timeliest method to monitor public communication and media coverage to gauge reaction to your message and make necessary modifications.

Readers who were in the New York City area on September 11, 2001 can probably offer their own testimony about the survivability of the Internet. The attacks on the World Trade Center caused widespread problems as people encountered difficulties in trying to get a dial tone on their hard-wired or wireless telephones. Although it became nearly impossible to place calls, it was possible for people with DSL access or cable modems or dedicated connections in their offices to get onto the Internet to seek sources of information.

Our second bulleted point could be summarized as "Internet as teleprompter." In a time of crisis, it is important to coordinate a company-wide response that can be followed by executives and other employees who might be interviewed at facilities around the country or around the globe. Using an intranet site or a "secret" URL on the public Internet to post your communications strategy provides everyone with a document to which they can refer to keep themselves "on message."

The Internet's ability to change by the minute is clearly a strength in a time of crisis and offers you the ability to let employees, employees' families, customers, stockholders, and reporters keep up with the latest news from you while you keep up with their latest articles or broadcasts.

PLAN NOW

Companies and their PR representatives need to be thinking now about how they will respond to a crisis. Their responses will probably be very different depending on whether they're reacting to a factory explosion that threatens the lives of workers and nearby residents or to a financial audit that raises questions about the validity of past earnings reports. Such scenarios need to be worked through, so that everyone on the PR team knows what needs to happen when the crisis occurs. Some elements will be common to all responses and should be prepared in advance. For example, a crisis is likely to attract the interest of reporters who are less familiar with your company than those who cover the company on a regular basis. This means that a good, solid background on the company's history, its businesses, and its reputation should be front and center in any online resource area. A list of links to local, state, and federal government agencies can also be developed in advance of a crisis for easy reference when you want to direct Web site visitors to the Federal Emergency Management Agency, Environmental Protection Agency, or whatever agency is involved in your crisis. An FAQ file can be an important element that allows you to develop answers to the questions that you anticipate from reporters and others. It should save you from answering the same questions repeatedly and free up some time for you to gather and monitor all information that is reported and disseminated by the media. However, this is not, by any means, to say that the Internet replaces the human contact. The Internet is a buffer zone, which makes it easier on the CEO or the public relations team, but the CEO must still show leadership by being present and accessible. The bottom line: professionals still need to be available to personally answer questions that must be addressed especially those questions that extend beyond a company's Web site crisis area.

LESSONS FROM 9/11

The tragic events of September 11, 2001 again provide us with solid examples of how the Internet can be used effectively in time of crisis. As a first step, many companies posted news statements on their Web sites to address the disaster. These statements communicated a company's immediate actions and kept the public informed as these announcements were frequently updated. For instance, we saw many of the following types of statements: "XYZ company is doing everything possible to determine the damages to our company in New York City." Other statements addressed the number of people in a particular company who were in the World Trade Center working at the time of the terrorist attack. Numerous companies immediately set forth a strong statement from a CEO or chairman of the board that focused on their concern, their thoughts, and their prayers for every family who had a loved one unaccounted for at the time. In the days following the attacks, many companies released information on a daily basis in the form of a news release. These releases stressed the anguish over employee losses and the concern for those whose whereabouts were unknown. Finally, news releases offered counseling information for employees, family members, and friends of those affected by the disaster.

Of course, news releases were not the only method to keep up-to-date information available at a time when so many other channels of communications were not in proper working order. The interactive nature of the Internet shone through brightly, providing people with an opportunity to communicate with one another about their experiences, their fears, and their prayers. Many shared information about how others online could donate money and blood.

One company in particular stands out for the manner in which it used the Web for crisis management. Sandler O'Neill & Partners, L.P. certainly was not looking for any type of recognition when it developed its Family Support site on its company Web site (to view the Sandler O'Neill Family Support site go to *sandleroneill.com*, then click on the left-hand navigation button, Family Support). From the looks of the site, it did not take Sandler O'Neill long to see that it was imperative to communicate immediately, even prior to the confirmation of the loss of 66 employees of the company. On the Web site, Sandler O'Neill referred to these individuals as its partners, colleagues, and friends. There's a combination of reasons this site was so effective:

- **Easy functionality:** In a crisis, no one wants to be clicking around endlessly for information. The simple left-hand navigation bar contained important buttons, clearly marked for easy access that led to critical information. Examples of these buttons include Continuing Counseling, Office of the Chief Medical Examiner, Donation Information, Sandler O'Neill Assistance Foundation, Memorial Service Information, Press Releases, and News Coverage.

- **Updated information:** The Web site is visibly documented with its most recent update (e.g., "Last Updated: Wednesday, May 29th at 10:00 AM EDT"). For example, on May 29, 2002, the Web site let the families of Sandler O'Neill employees know abut the May 30 World Trade Center ceremonies. Prominently displayed was information on the times that the viewing areas were open, the location of family entrances, as well as the details for a June 2, 2002 gathering and mass.

- **Forthright statements and early answers:** Sandler O'Neill was quick to move forward with statements regarding company losses, direction of company operations, continuing family outreach programs, active search programs for missing employees, and announcements of the company's intention to "open" for business within the first several days after the attack. Such statements are particularly useful to the news media that are seeking information portals to guide them with their coverage of the crisis. In addition, employees, families, and many other groups connected to Sandler O'Neill relied on the released information on a daily basis.

- **One channel and one voice:** Although company officials always must be available in a crisis, it appears that the Sandler O'Neill Web site was a strong communication vehicle that housed information clearly enough to answer many of the daily crisis questions. The Web site truly communicated a sense of calm, direction, and confidence on behalf of the company. The material released via the Web site was well coordinated and controlled in a situation that was one of the most chaotic in American history. The Sandler O'Neill site spoke of credibility and concern and acted as a single spokesperson that communicated a united company front from the CEO to the senior executives to the rest of the company.

- **News coverage made simple and accessible:** On the Sandler O'Neill site, it was evident that PR professionals were busy searching for any type of media coverage that mentioned the company. The media coverage varied from the op-ed contribution titled, "The Damaged Spirit of the September 11 Fund" in *The New York Times* and the *Fortune* cover story "Starting Over" to the *60 Minutes* interview on CBS that discussed how Sandler O'Neill would take the necessary steps forward to rebuild its company. Sandler O'Neill made it extremely easy for all of the stakeholders of the company to follow the positive communication to build hope and faith in a successful plan that would rebuild the firm.

United Airlines' use of the Internet in its response to the events of September 11 has also been well chronicled. John Kiker, United's vice president of worldwide communications, told the *Holmes Report* how the airline worked with Fleishman-Hillard to react quickly to the hijackings and destruction of two of its planes—one at the World Trade Center and one in Pennsylvania.

Kiker said that United put its crisis plan into effect with 40 to 50 of his staffers handling phones in a crisis center to respond to media inquiries. Other staffers canceled the airline's scheduled advertisements and still others were detailed to employee communications, which involved sending e-mail and voice mail to a workforce of 100,000 that includes more than 30,000 pilots and flight attendants not situated in an office setting. He said Fleishman-Hillard concentrated on monitoring media reports so that United could attempt to correct any incorrect reports.

Kiker told the *Holmes Report* that he believes the three Cs are important to crisis management: compassion, cooperation, and contact. "We have to show our compassion for the families of the victims," he said. "We also have to make the point that we are cooperating with the relevant authorities, which in most cases means the FAA, but in this case included the FBI," he noted. "Finally, we have to make sure that people know how to contact us, and where they can go for the latest information."

United's Web site played a key role in getting information out to the media and to employees and the families of passengers. The company's press release archive shows it issued six releases in a period of less than seven hours on September 11. E-mail and the *ual.com* Web site helped bring the releases to thousands of people. Each statement included a quote from CEO James Goodwin, who was also involved in communicating with the airline's employees and with families of the crash victims. Each statement dominated a simple black-and-white Web page, free of its usual links about ticket sales. The only links on the page were to a list of other releases issued that day, fact sheets about the company and its airplanes, and the Web sites of partners such as Boeing.

American Airlines, which also lost two flights on that tragic day, took a simple approach to the design of its crisis Web site. Its home page at *aa.com* was simply the text of a statement from the airline with links offered to the regular *aa.com* Web site and to the site of parent company AMR Corporation for Web visitors seeking more information about the day's events. (Copies of the *aa.com* and *ual.com* sites as they looked on September 11, 2001 were available at *web.archive.org* the last time we checked.)

The events of September 11 had a less tragic and more indirect impact on Massachusetts-based Dunkin' Donuts, which also provided a good demonstration of how the Internet could be used effectively to get the company's message out quickly in a time of crisis. It was only hours after the terrorist attacks on New York City and Washington, DC, that e-mails were flooding into Dunkin' Donuts' corporate offices. The e-mails, by the nature of the allegation, were extremely damaging to the brand. Many of the complaints inundating the Dunkin' Donuts PR team stemmed from an unverified incident in one of the company's franchises in Cedar Grove, New Jersey. The unfounded complaint stated that a U.S. flag was burned in celebration of the attack on the United States. Another account related to another Dunkin' Donuts operation in a small town in New Jersey where an American flag was seen on the floor with Arabic writing on it. The news was spreading quickly and e-mails rallied support for an immediate nationwide boycott of Dunkin' Donuts. These e-mails pleaded with any and all persons who patronized a Dunkin' Donuts franchise. The messages urged Dunkin' Donuts' customers not to purchase anything from the company, as it was anti-American. In addition, complaints also focused on how Dunkin' Donuts was not doing its part to help out at the Ground Zero disaster site when many other restaurants were providing police officers and firefighters with food and drinks. Dunkin' Donuts recognized that it had to counteract the negative rumors before its business was seriously affected.

Because the Internet was the main source of the allegations, that's where Dunkin' Donuts began its campaign to halt the false allegations about the company. Dunkin' Donuts began its response by contacting the Cedar Grove store to question the owners and store employees and review video footage of the day's events to get to the bottom of the allegations. Approximately 40 people were questioned in the process to find out that not one person could confirm the actual complaint against the company. As a matter of fact, Dunkin' Donuts' public relations firm did its best to get to the bottom of the incident by asking employees if they had seen the incident as a firsthand account. Apparently in the effort to uncover the truth, all but two of the questioned employees stated that the account was not seen personally. There were two people who said they did witness the alleged account but could not pinpoint or provide concrete information to verify the complaint.

Dunkin' Donuts' response to the rumors took the form of an e-mail campaign that was directed toward all of the individuals who originally contacted them regarding the supposed incident with a request for them to forward on the company's e-mail to anyone who they knew. The company's e-mail noted that during times of crisis it's often difficult not to react with emotion. In fact, the correspondence stressed that people, in general, should be more sensitive and conscious about persons of different races, cultures, and religions. Dunkin' Donuts also took a very strong stance against the alleged action, stating that the company denounced any of the acts reported. It wasn't long before many of the consumers sent letters of apology to Dunkin' Donuts. The company had successfully demonstrated that it had the know-how to use the Internet as a quick and reliable source of communication to slow the speed of the rumors on the Internet and eventually bring the negative publicity to a halt.

The Dunkin' Donuts incident and the company's effective response to it was written about in *The Wall Street Journal*, as was the story of a much smaller establishment beset by negative rumors related to September 11. The Sheik, a Middle Eastern restaurant in Orchard Lake, Michigan, unfortunately did not respond to the negative publicity as effectively after an e-mail was circulated on September 11 that stated that employees of the restaurant were cheering. The bottom line was that Americans should cease business at The Sheik and that all Americans should forward the e-mail to all of their contacts. The owner of The Sheik tried to react quickly by telephoning customers to reject the allegations and by placing American flags in the windows of his restaurant. He even went so far as to ask his employees not to speak in Arabic when in the presence of customers. However, the e-mail spread with far greater speed than the restaurant owner could dial the phone and business fell by more than 50 percent before ultimately rebounding.

A QUICK RESPONSE

As we noted earlier, the crises companies face are not always on the scale of the September 11 attacks or the crippling revelations from Enron and Worldcom in recent years.

PR people also need to be ready to respond to events that carry the threat of simple embarrassment. Such was the case for a northeastern newspaper group that cosponsored a debate among Congressional candidates in recent years. Hours before the well-publicized debate among four candidates for a Congressional seat in the Northeast, a fifth candidate circulated a less-than-flattering news release demanding to be included in the event. The news release featured words like "disgrace" and "embarrassment" and included a threat to contact each of the other four candidates to ask them to withdraw from the newspaper's debate.

The PR agency needed to act quickly. The media was already e-mailing with inquiries regarding the debate and the embarrassing oversight. Questions and eyebrows were swiftly being raised with respect to the situation. The PR agency, in no time at all, drafted an e-mail statement that addressed the oversight and the newspaper's regret over the situation. The e-mail was distributed to all the media representatives that were inquiring about the incident. Next, the PR agency reached out to the fifth candidate immediately to invite him to participate in the debate. The fifth candidate gladly accepted the invitation.

Even after the tensions were eased between the newspaper group and the fifth candidate, crisis management was not over. The PR agency realized by the number of telephone calls and e-mails regarding the situation that the wildfire was still spreading on the Internet. The PR professionals began searching and monitoring all Internet communication for statements regarding the situation on various news Web sites and political portals. A number of Web sites were criticizing the newspaper group even after the situation was rectified. However, the beauty of the Internet allows PR professionals to alter communication quickly with updated postings. The PR agency was able to approach all of the news outlets directly through e-mail to combat the negative PR and to provide the outlets with the current information that they could verify through the fifth candidate's campaign office. The e-mail statement was distributed to all the Web site editors along with another statement updating the situation to let the media outlets know that the fifth candidate received an invitation to participate. The PR agency was able to monitor site after site, and then see how the information changed to reflect the current situation (altering the negative to the positive). Years ago, this type of quick reversal in a crisis situation would have been unheard of. This situation was back to normal within a two-hour time frame as a result of an effective e-mail statement and the close monitoring of communication. The Internet and the quick thinking of skilled professionals who acted quickly in crisis-management mode were responsible for the successful outcome.

PLANNING A CRISIS SITE

The examples previously cited regarding Sandler O'Neill, United Airlines, and American Airlines illustrate the tremendous value in using your company's Web site to respond quickly to a crisis. This might mean having a plan to address a major event on the home page without affecting the overall appearance and functionality of the rest of the site. This is the path that Worldcom chose in June 2002 when it disclosed massive accounting irregularities. It placed a black box on its home page that contained links to a press release and to a Webcast of remarks by CEO John Sidgmore. The rest of the home page continued to feature links to Worldcom's service offerings, its corporate information, and career center.

In many cases, however, your company might want to follow the airlines' model of September 11 and plan to have a crisis Web site that acknowledges the severity of a situation and indicates that the company is responding in a necessary fashion to a fire, an explosion, a chemical leak, a shooting rampage, and so on. Being proactive in the age of the Internet means having more than a plan on paper. Actual Web pages, known as *ghost templates* should be created so that they can be turned on and made accessible on the Internet when crises occur.

Some solid principles for designing and implementing ghost templates include these:

- PR professionals should establish a relationship with the IT department before a crisis occurs.

- The design of the crisis site should be predetermined.
- The IT department should be responsible for programming an administration area with prebuilt templates.
- The prebuilt or ghost template should be designed by the IT team and updated by the PR team in accordance with their crisis plan.
- PR people should access the prebuilt templates through a password-protected administrative section to update the crisis Web site daily.
- The data entered into the prebuilt template should be submitted by the PR person to the draft site.
- IT people can program the draft Web site to be secure so that information transmitted over the Internet is in an encrypted format.
- A draft crisis site mirrors (or is identical to) the live site and is used during the preapproval process.

We mentioned earlier in the book that PR professionals must get acquainted with their IT department. When it comes to crisis management, it's imperative that the relationship is already in place before the unexpected occurs. PR people need to work with Web programmers to start understanding how a crisis Web site comes to fruition. We spoke to a few programmers at different full-service agencies who all confirmed the same information and broke down the process in layman's terms. By working closely with programmers, PR professionals can use their crisis management plans on the Internet more effectively. In our efforts to obtain fixed pricing for the different types of crisis Web sites, various programmers informed us that these sites could range in price from $5,000 to $50,000, depending on the nature and scope of the crisis and the number of categories or areas of information on the site. In an effort to determine a price, the first step is to decide how many categories are needed. For instance, a crisis site could have several categories including, but not limited to the following (see Figure 11-1):

1. President's or CEO's message—updated daily.
2. Press releases—announcements on behalf of the company.

3. News coverage—news on the Web collected by the PR team.

4. Employee support section—support information for all parties involved in the crisis.

5. Emergency contacts—telephone numbers and e-mail addresses for further information.

6. Extra category—perhaps, two to three extra categories depending on the nature of the crisis.

These categories are considered the first level because they are found on the home page of the crisis site (usually on a navigation bar). The subsequent level or levels would be the content in each of the named categories. The PR team has to think about how a crisis in its industry would affect the company and design a Web site with as many categories and levels as necessary to make sure that the media, employees, customers, and shareholders can get the information that they are seeking.

After the PR team selects the site categories and designs a schematic of the site's architecture, it's time for the Web programmers to become involved. It's their job to make sure the

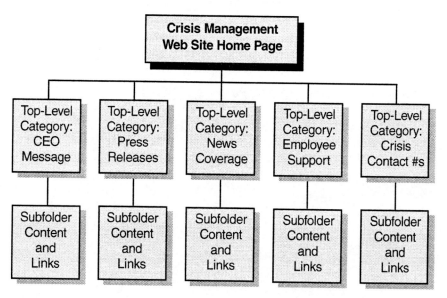

FIGURE 11-1   Schematic of Crisis Web Site. Flowchart designed by Vinny Cozzi, PFS Markeywyse.

site is as easy to use as possible for both the PR team updating the site and the public that logs on to view the information. The Web programmer creates an administration site that contains all of the templates for content input. The PR team enters all of the crisis information into premade forms or templates. A ghost template is created for each category in the site. For instance, in a News Coverage section of a crisis Web site, the Web programmers might build a template that asks the PR person to enter data in the following fields:

- Title of article
- Date published
- Author's name
- Brief description of the article
- Link to article's Web site

As illustrated by the flowchart in Figure 11-2, PR professionals can continuously update the data by logging into the administration area, which is password protected and encrypted. This area allows them to either enter initial information or update existing documents. They can then choose to make the changes immediately on the live site or make them only on a draft site that must be reviewed by a crisis team before the changes can take effect on the live site. The draft site is a valuable crisis management tool that enables the PR team to set the categories in place and get the Web site pages ready for the content that follows. What's most important is that the PR team has full control over the structure of the crisis site and over the mechanism for updating and reviewing the content on it. With all of the discussion regarding crises and the need to provide quick and accurate information to the public, you might be wondering what type of bandwidth is necessary to facilitate up to 10 to 15 times the normal amount of traffic on a company's Web site. We spoke with Interland, Inc., a provider of Web hosting services for small to medium-sized businesses, and learned that most of its service offerings offer unlimited bandwidth should more be required during unusual circumstances like an unexpected crisis. We suggest that you speak with your Web hosting service or your client's service provider to assure yourself that additional bandwidth will be easy to obtain when the unexpected occurs.

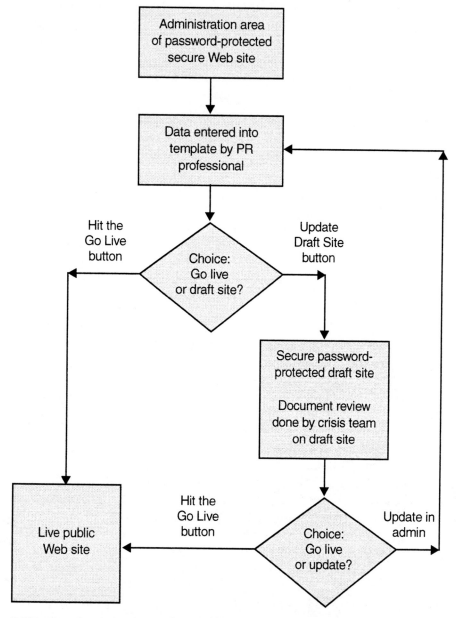

FIGURE 11-2   User Choice Flowchart. Flowchart designed by Vinny Cozzi, PFS Markeywyse.

We've only briefly touched on how building an online crisis management site is helpful to the media. The media need to find information that's current and accurate as they cover a crisis situation. The manner in which the media gathers information has changed drastically since the inception of the World Wide Web. One business reporter, Joe Perone of *The Star-Ledger* of Newark, New Jersey, has been writing for more than 20 years. He's handled crises pre- and post-Internet and shared with us his insights on how the Internet is used effectively by the media. (See our following interview with Perone in this chapter.)

In our next chapter, we discuss the importance of making sure your online communications plan is integrated with your offline plan, and how important it is to thread together many of the strategies that we've discussed in the chapters thus far.

MEDIA INTERVIEW:
JOE PERONE OF *THE STAR LEDGER*

"Back in the days of the Johnson & Johnson Tylenol crisis, we were lucky if we had fax machines," recalled Joe Perone, a business reporter for *The Star-Ledger* of Newark, New Jersey, and a 20-year veteran in the field of journalism. "We had information transmitted over the wire, but it's hardly what you could call instantaneous analyst reports," he explained.

Perone was one of the reporters who covered the 1982 product tampering crisis that left seven users of Extra-Strength Tylenol dead from cyanide poisoning. The major difference he described between then and now is the Internet. Perone gave a detailed account of what it was like to be a reporter in the early 1980s. He described his earlier days as a journalist as "so much slower . . . almost the Stone Age." One very important point that he stressed during the interview was that as technology advances, jobs change. Journalists who are normally on tight deadlines are expected to handle more as a result of the Internet. Simply put, "We're working harder to produce better stories." Perone described the Internet like the early development of the American railroad system. Using this simile, he suggested that just as railroads were instrumental to American industry, the Internet was critical to making America an information superpower.

In addition to covering the Johnson & Johnson crisis, Perone also reported on the 1984 Union Carbide chemical leak in Bhopal, India that killed nearly 4,000 people and disabled many others. "If Union Carbide had the Internet at the time of its crisis," he stated, "the company would have reacted much more quickly than it did." Unfortunately, the CEO waited too long, appearing indifferent to the public. In the case of Union Carbide, had executives in the United States been given information in a timely fashion, they would have responded in kind.

These are Perone's final words with regard to how journalists use the Web in a crisis situation:

- Even though we have the Internet, that doesn't mean that everyone knows how to use it.

- The Internet is the great equalizer. It's continually changing, as are the journalists who use it.

- In a crisis situation, journalists don't solely rely on the Internet. They use both the Internet and the telephone for human contact.

- Human contact will never go away because you can't fax or e-mail a relationship, especially during a crisis.

- Building the relationship with the media certainly helps before the crisis strikes. Chances are that if there's a relationship in place, the media will already know it's dealing with a company that has proven itself to be a straight shooter.

- Crisis management is not an exact science, but that's what separates the great inside PR teams from the "clueless" ones.

- If a company doesn't have a good ear for reading the public or the investment community, then it doesn't matter which communication tool it chooses. ■

12 INTEGRATING YOUR PR STRATEGIES.

➤ A client's online and offline PR messages need to be consistent in language, tone, and design.
➤ Strategies can be integrated without the need for a huge budget.
➤ Integrating the Internet into your campaign enhances feedback.

Are there any communication plans or marketing campaigns implemented by PR professionals that do not involve the Internet in some manner? It would be unusual in this day and age for a company not to have a Web site of some kind, an e-mailed announcement, or even a Webcast of a major announcement, but are these Internet efforts truly integrated with the overall PR or marketing campaign?

In our experience, the answer to that question is too often no. Even in these early days of the 21st Century, we still see press releases issued with references to Web site features that are impossible to locate. Clearly, someone wrote the release with the expectation that the supporting documentation would be online by the time the release was issued, but something went wrong somewhere. Sometimes a release will direct you to the front page of a company's site, where there will be no clues of how to find out more about the news in the release. Other times, a release will include a lengthy URL like *abccompany.com/2003/announcements/category/productname.html* that appears to be designed especially for the announcement in question, but produces a 404 error when you try to connect to the page.

The problem seems to be that the PR people too frequently are not on the same page as the people in charge of a company's Web site. We argued strenuously in Chapter 6 for strong cooperation between the PR folks and the Web site managers when it comes to getting documents placed quickly in online newsrooms. We'll reiterate that plea here because close cooperation is so important to integrated communications. If PR people are not confident that the Web site managers will post documents by a specified time, those documents should not be promised by a certain time to reporters, shareholders, and other constituents. Such promises risk creating a frustrating experience for your constituents and an embarrassing situation for your client.

Beyond the coordination issues, PR people must take pains to make sure they are including a consistent message in the materials they make available in paper-based press kits, online press materials, marketing materials, and advertising. Although it is certainly okay—and often advisable—to modify a message to get the desired response from different market segments, the various efforts need to fit together into a cohesive strategy. For example, a company that knows its Web site is most popular with its youngest consumers might accompany a new product announcement with online games or contests. This is a good way to leverage the capabilities of the Internet, but care must be taken to ensure that the online features have the same look and feel that is included in other PR materials for the product announcement.

Whether campaign objectives are meant to change an opinion, evoke an action, or increase awareness, the messages that the PR team has strategically developed through each of the selected channels must be consistent in meaning, carry the same tone, and bear a design that looks and feels similar to the other channels utilized. Through integration, the channels must work together with supportive communication and collectively create more of an impact to enhance the company's messages.

Pepsi-Cola Company is an example of a large company with numerous offline promotions that are well integrated with Pepsi's Web site (*pepsi.com*). Pepsi's strategy is to create a connection with its consumers that can be strengthened by logging onto the company's Web site. In 2002, the soda maker hitched itself to the rising star of singer Britney Spears, connecting itself to a popular entertainer and offering Spears' fans an opportunity to find out more about her concert tour. Early in the year, Pepsi unveiled commercials starring Spears for the Super Bowl and teamed up with Yahoo! in a promotion that asked Yahoo! members to log on to the Pepsi Web site to vote for the best Spears' commercials. The commercials subsequently became part of a large area on the Pepsi site devoted to Spears and her "Dream Within a Dream Tour 2002," which offered everything from concert dates and locations to a photo album, e-cards, and a sweepstakes.

A consumer who found Spears mentioned on a Pepsi bottle cap or on a poster in a music store had no trouble finding her when he or she arrived at the Pepsi Web site. Oversized graphics on the front page of the site directed users to Pepsi's various promotions, which also included the Austin Powers film *Goldmember* and Major League Soccer in the summer of 2002.

Once inside the Britney Buzz area, it was obvious that all of Pepsi's advertising and promotion behind Britney Spears and her relationship with the company was consistent right down to the graphics on the site and the fun spirit of the campaign. Pepsi showed us how offline and online promotions integrate well. It's not hard to imagine that Spears fans that might have heard about a new concert date in a radio or TV news report would have immediately checked the Pepsi Web site for more information.

Pursuing an integrated strategy also helped Pepsi with its objective of collecting as much data as possible about its audience and about Pepsi drinkers (which ultimately leads to building better relationships). By driving people to the Web site and asking them to share information, Pepsi was reported to have compiled a list of more than 500,000 e-mail addresses.[1]

INTEGRATION TIPS

Of course, we realize that not every company is Pepsi-Cola, nor does every company have the ability to build a Web site like Pepsi's World. However, we do believe that Pepsi has done several things right on its Web site—many of which can be emulated even by those on a smaller budget. They include the following:

- **Graphics:** Graphics must be easily recognizable icons to click on for more information. These graphics should resemble the visuals used in conjunction with other communication channels.

- **Contact information:** Having contact information up front and available offers a Web visitor the ability to contact a PR person to ask questions or discuss questions that are not answered on a Web site. In addition, companies can create online forms for Web visitors who want more information. The user can be asked to fill out the form and hit Submit, and can then be contacted by a representative of the company who is equipped with more information. Forms that ask for demographic information of the online visitors along with their e-mail addresses can end up as leads in the company's database. (We talk more in the next chapter about the need to disclose to the site's users what you are going to do with their personal data.)

- **Updated FAQs:** An updated file of FAQs is necessary to reflect a company's current campaign and to possibly answer questions that are not covered by the other communication channels.

---

1. *Business* 2.0 (March 22, 2002).

- **Banners:** Banners can be shared between campaign sponsors to illustrate the involvement of various companies. Banners are easily recognizable and can be clicked on for more information to enhance the broad reach and involvement of many parties.

- **News releases:** News release postings can certainly offer updated information to any party (not just the media) interested in the most recent company news.

- **Language:** The language used on the Web site should contain the same message and tone of the language used in other channels, whether it's radio, television, billboards, direct mail, and so on.

- **Design:** Web site design is very important to capture an audience's attention with a design that is already visually recognizable and accepted. If the design of the site and the overall look and feel on the Web site are not familiar or do not mimic what's presented in other communication channels, audiences tend to become confused and disinterested and they might not embrace the company's communication presented on the Web.

- **Data:** Companies can track data regarding the habits of their visitors on the Web and analyze those numbers to gauge the amount of interest in a campaign. They can also review user demographic information from a Web tracking report.

FITTING TOOLS TOGETHER

Having an integrated PR campaign means that each new tool that you use must be carefully inserted into the campaign in a way that keeps the look and feel of the campaign consistent. This means that the tools we urged you to implement in earlier chapters (online newsrooms, e-mail pitches, e-newsletters, Webcasts) should not be added to a campaign in a haphazard way just to try them out or to get your feet wet.

The online newsroom, for example, must be part of an integrated strategy to provide the media and other groups with the ability to find answers to their questions. Reporters who figure out that the roster of a company's top executives listed in its online newsroom is out of date and that the "latest releases" are actually a month old are going to have a low opinion of the company and not become frequent users of that pressroom.

At the same time, PR people should not undercut their own efforts by trying to be too fancy with the newsroom technology. It is not recommended, for example, that a press release offer a "sneak preview" of a new automobile model provided that the reporter has the necessary password for a particular area of a car maker's Web site. Such tricks might make some chosen journalists feel special, but they could also exclude busy journalists from major publications who are reluctant to jump through hoops. They might therefore give less ink to your new car model than they devote to those of your competitors. Your message across all media needs to be one of openness and accessibility. If you go to the trouble to communicate something new and exciting, use the Web to further promote the effort. Don't make it difficult for the people who are interested in publicizing something on your behalf.

Similarly, the e-mail pitches we recommended in Chapter 7 and the e-mail newsletters we championed in Chapter 8 must be well integrated with the rest of your PR campaign. Any logos or icons used in the press release or newsletter should be consistent with those the reporter or consumer will find when he or she visits your Web site. All verbal information must also be consistent in tone and content regardless of whether it is in the hard-copy press kit, in an e-mail, in a newsletter, or on the Web site. You do not want inconsistencies that could be confusing to reporters and consumers and produce more questions for you to answer. Remember, your job is to build relationships with people by helping them do their jobs more easily.

One other tool we recommended—the crisis management Web site—also must not be forgotten in your integration efforts. You cannot create a ghost template for a crisis management Web site and let it get dusty on a hard drive somewhere.

It needs to be updated regularly to make sure that when it is needed it will feature the latest icons and other elements that make it integrate well with your regular Web site, press releases, hard-copy press kits, and other PR tools.

WHEN INTEGRATION WORKS

As the Internet matures, more PR teams are integrating their online and offline efforts and the results are frequently impressive. For today's PR professionals, we see the lines of marketing and public relations blurring. With tight budgets in a slow economy, especially, we find that professionals are taking advantage of PR and marketing promotion together to maximize campaign efforts. PR people are becoming more involved with promotional sweepstakes, contests, charity events, and so on. These next few examples move away from the traditional integrated PR on the Web focusing on news releases, pressrooms, and newsletters. Instead, we see more examples of integration on a daily basis in brand packaging, television commercials that drive traffic to the Internet, and radio programming. A case in point is provided by the women-oriented Web site iVillage and the Pepperidge Farms brand of cookies. In one promotion, a consumer of Pepperidge Farm Milano cookies encountered a small card that referenced iVillage when he or she first opened the cookie package. The card invited the customer to log onto the iVillage site to discover other pleasures (similar to the pleasure of eating a Pepperidge Farm Milano cookie) including "soothing tips" and "serene screensavers." A Milano Moment icon at the bottom of iVillage's home page made the content easy to find. The Milano Moment page loaded with the sounds of a bird chirping and offered not only screensavers, but also a chance to win a Spa Escape Sweepstakes for two. The brands were tied together by a message that stressed that everyone needs a little time to enjoy and indulge in the simple pleasures in life.

Motion picture studios might be the leaders when it comes to integrating the Internet into their PR and marketing strategies. Nearly every movie made in the last few years has been advertised with a URL where prospective moviegoers can see clips of the movie, biographies of the stars, and other information. Movies targeted at children seem to offer the most full-featured Web sites, often supplementing the clips with songs and interactive games, as was the case with Disney's *Lilo & Stitch* in 2002 (*disney.com/stitch*) and Disney and Pixar's *Monsters, Inc.* (*monstersrinc.com*) in 2001.

Finally, an example of radio advertising and Web integration is provided by Olive Crest's charity event held each year at CBS Television Studios on July 4. Olive Crest is an organization in Southern California that helps in the prevention of child abuse. Because it's estimated that every year millions of children are reported victims of child abuse and neglect, and that number increases annually, Olive Crest holds this charity event annually to raise awareness and money for the organization.[2]

Before the event, KZLA, a local radio station in Southern California, publicized the charity event and urged people to log onto the Olive Crest Web site to watch a live Webcast available through JVC's latest broadcast-quality, handheld camcorder, and to make donations to the charity via the Web site. The Web site, *forolivecrest.com*, was designed as a part of an integrated campaign to create enhanced awareness for the July 4 event. In addition, other methods to integrate the communication on the Internet included the following:

- E-mail blasts to the media (trade, consumer, and newspapers)

- HTML reminder e-mail invitations and messages to invite interested parties to the *forolivecrest.com* Web site

- Links and banners on all of the sponsors' Web sites for easy access to the July 4 event

- Archived streaming video for online users to view if they missed the actual event

---

2.   Olive Crest was a client of Deirdre's firm, PFS Marketwyse, in 2002.

BEYOND CONSISTENCY

Although consistency is a major reason to make sure you have a well-rounded, integrated PR campaign on and off the Internet, we should not leave this chapter without at least mentioning some of the side benefits of building an online segment to your campaign.

- **Repetition:** Being redundant is usually thought of as a bad thing. However, when it comes to communication and the ability to integrate messages on the Internet, redundancy is a key strategy. Especially when it comes to branding or image building, repetition is often the key to a message being received, interpreted, and then retained. Today's marketing world is more crowded then it has ever been. Too many messages heard daily are selectively discarded or just filtered out with the rest of the communication noise. With repetition a visitor is able to recognize a company's message more easily, whether the redundancy is the spoken word, the written word, or visuals. As a result of advanced Internet technology, all three types of reinforced communication—spoken, written, and visual—can be achieved via HTML text, audiovisuals, and streaming video or Webcasts.

- **Dynamic visuals and audio:** The Internet is a wonderful channel that allows us to utilize live or streaming video to capture a moment in time. Web audio and visuals have come a long way and will continue to improve as technology produces better Webcasts and streaming video for audiences who are not able to attend an event.

- **Audience reach:** PR professionals choose to integrate the Internet into communication programs because we know that more and more users of different ages, education levels, religions, genders, and races are online each day. As PR professionals, we're seeing that many of our audiences are enjoying the Internet and are beginning to trust it as a good source of accurate information. As more audiences spend their time online at work or at home through faster connections (DSL lines or better) as we discussed in Chapter 2, it's important to catch their attention when we can. This does not necessarily mean that we have to use annoying Web advertising that pops up on the screen and interferes with the reading of Web content. In fact it is better to deliver clear, consistent messages as part of the Web content to get site users interested in a company's product or service. In addition, we've noted earlier in this book that journalists are online, sometimes using the Internet as their first source for research on a company. The Internet is capturing our most important audiences, which is significant as the world continues to become more and more media saturated.

In our next chapter, we tackle what you need to know about privacy online—an increasingly important topic that is sure to trip up Internet users who are not willing to pay it proper attention.

PR INTERVIEW: ELISA PADILLA, MANAGER, EVENTS & ATTRACTIONS GROUP, NATIONAL BASKETBALL ASSOCIATION

Question: In your experience, what does the Internet bring in terms of value/benefits to a PR/marketing campaign?

Padilla: The Internet offers convenience to consumers. Convenience is a benefit that consumers appreciate based on hectic schedules and fast-paced life. In developing the micro site—*nba.yahoo.com*—our goal was to provide our fans with a vehicle where they could obtain information on our program at all times. In all marketing and public relations information, collateral materials, the call to action directs consumers to *nba.yahoo.com*. The micro site is used as a tool to provide fans with the most current information on the NBA's basketball and music tour.

Question: What's the best integrated campaign that you've seen recently?

Padilla: The best integrated campaign I have seen recently was for Washington Mutual, which sought to highlight its services as a lending institution. The "YES—stamp" campaign included outdoor advertising, TV, radio, and Internet marketing. The campaign was designed as a comprehensive campaign with a consistent look and messaging across all media properties. Consumers were directed to log on to *washingtonmutual.com* for additional information on lending services.

Question: In your opinion, are PR/marketing professionals utilizing the Internet as much as they could for integrated campaigns?

Padilla: In my humble opinion, marketing/PR professionals do not use the Internet to the fullest capacity as part of integrated campaigns. Depending on the company's objectives and product, companies vary with the capabilities of promoting their products on the Internet.

Question: Can you give us an example (it can be hypothetical) of a campaign that would have produced better results if it included Internet marketing and PR strategies?

Padilla: The U.S. Postal Service is an example of a company that could produce far better results if it included the Internet into its marketing efforts. Consumers use the Internet for convenience and to save time. It is used as a one-stop-shopping vehicle to get products, service, and, most importantly, convenience. Recently when the price of stamps increased, consumers were forced to purchase the new priced stamps. The day of the increase, the Postal Service Web site "crashed" as a result of the demand from consumers trying to purchase stamps.

Question: Moving forward, do you eventually see more online strategy integrated into marketing/PR campaigns?

Padilla: I definitely think that companies understand more and more that consumers want convenience. Companies will integrate the Internet into marketing plans more and more because we're faced with the reality that the Internet is not going away. ■

Question: In your experience, what does the Internet bring in terms of value/benefits to a PR/marketing campaign?

Miletsky: The Internet brings the same to a PR/marketing event that it brings to the general population—speed and instant access to information. Regardless of specific benchmarks, every marketing or PR effort shares a common goal: increased visibility and interest among its target market. The Internet allows that interest to be fed immediately. The "real-time" aspect of information (whether the target market in this case is a journalist, broadcaster, or end user) supports a campaign by turning a vague interest in a company, product, or service, into a timely need.

"Good" marketers have begun to include their Web address in practically all of their material, including advertising, direct mail, and press releases. "Great" marketers realize in advance the type of information people will be looking for based on their campaign, and adjust their Web site accordingly.

Question: What's the best integrated campaign (must include PR) that you've seen recently?

Miletsky: BMW is one of the best marketers around when it comes to the Internet. In almost a backward PR program, their work with the Web generated an unbelievable amount of press coverage, which in turn sent more people back to their site.

Taking advantage of the multimedia aspects that the Web offers, BMW created BMW Films—an entity focused on producing short, fictionalized movies that would play on BMW's Web site. Each movie involved a BMW car, and each had a big Hollywood name like Madonna attached to it, either as a star or as a director. The PR generated from that effort, along with a simultaneous co-op advertising promotion with VH-1, was a brilliantly integrated effort that really struck a chord with its market.

Question: In your opinion, are PR professionals utilizing the Internet as much as they could for integrated campaigns?

Miletsky: Flatly, no. Marketers who haven't yet figured out how to harness it vastly underutilize the innate power of the Web. Cyber newsrooms, for example, are blatantly missing from a large number of sites—most amazingly from sites that believe in and undertake PR strategies. But the worst mistake companies make is forgetting that the Web is not static—it can be changed, edited, and updated relatively quickly. In addition, vast amounts of content can be provided for absolutely no cost (except the time it takes to compile and upload).

Strategists don't know this, however. Their limitations in terms of programming keep them from taking full advantage of the Web in their overall marketing efforts.

Question: Can you give us an example (it can be hypothetical) of a campaign that would have produced better results if it included the Internet marketing and PR strategies?

Miletsky: Suppose for example, that Company X is introducing a new product and making an aggressive marketing push for that product, using advertising, plus promotional and public relations strategies. When the interest of the market gets piqued, a person's first impulse is to find out more on the Web site. The home page, then, should feature that new product prominently to support the overall campaign. Remarkably, however, many marketers neglect this aspect of the campaign, even though it's one of the most important parts. In most cases, Company X would continue to feature its standard home page, forcing the user to search for the newly marketed product. Even worse, some marketers might have neglected their sites to the point that the new product information isn't even available at the time of the campaign.

The point is that the Web needs to be considered at the very start of any integrated campaign, and prepared for in advance—not as an afterthought.

Question: Moving forward, do you eventually see more online strategy integrated into marketing/PR campaigns?

Miletsky: Yes, but only to an extent. There will be an increase in some Internet marketing elements, such as opt-in e-mail blasts, but I think we're still a long way away from utilizing the Web to its full potential. Marketers continue to debate the pros and cons of banner advertising as a brand vehicle, while refusing to embrace the real value of the Internet—the site itself. Driving people to a site isn't the toughest part of marketing—the trick is to get the most out of each visitor once he or she is there.

The unfortunate reality is that there is a severe disconnect between the communications professionals and the programmers. Strategists don't know a lot about programming, and therefore they tend to underutilize the Web because they're afraid of it. When that fear is erased, and the gap between strategist and programmer is reduced, *then* we'll start to see the Internet being used more effectively. ∎

13 DON'T FORGET ABOUT PRIVACY

> ➤ Insufficient attention to privacy is a recipe for a PR mess.
> ➤ PR people should encourage clients to post honest privacy policies.
> ➤ Sites collecting information from children need to be particularly careful.
> ➤ U.S. sites can seek "safe haven" under European Union privacy rules.

Throughout this book, we've argued that the Internet can build on your existing PR strategies in ways not possible in the old, offline world. The added abilities to target messages, to deliver them quickly, and to maintain a newsroom that is open 24/7 can all be achieved without huge costs. One significant drawback of the Internet is the speed with which it can circulate negative news about your clients. Another downside, which we tackle in this chapter, is the demand that it places on you and your clients to construct policies governing your use of consumer information. Creating such policies was probably a worthwhile practice in the pre-Internet world to guide you in deciding what you might do with databases of names and addresses. However, in the Internet age, such policies have become imperative. Whether you're simply collecting reporters' e-mail addresses for press release distribution or helping your client administer an online questionnaire intended to record the shopping habits of site visitors, you need to be thinking long and hard about privacy practices.

For whatever reason, many people around the world are very concerned about what happens with information that they provide to Web sites. Perhaps they've heard stories about identity theft or maybe there's just a discomfort that people feel when they are plugging personal information into a Web form with no idea who is collecting that information or what they're doing with it. You could argue that your personal data are no less secure online than they are when you provide your credit card to a minimum-wage employee in a typical restaurant or discount store. However, such debates are purely academic and not worth your time. Today's reality is that people are clearly anxious about online data gathering and Web site operators need to do their best to allay those fears.

The United States, unlike many other countries, has taken a self-regulatory approach to online privacy with the Federal Trade Commission (FTC) in the lead role of encouraging Web sites to publish policies that tell their visitors what is done with their personal information. The early assessments of that approach were not exactly positive, as the FTC reported in June 1998 that a survey of 1,400 commercial Web sites had found that more than 85 percent of sites collected personal information, but only 14 percent posted any description of their information practices and only 2 percent had what the FTC considered to be a "comprehensive privacy policy."

A July 1999 report found some improvement, as a survey of 361 sites found 44 percent had posted privacy policies. The figure was up to 88 percent by the time of a May 2000 report, but the FTC used that report to push for policies that were more complete. It noted that only 20 percent of surveyed Web sites had embraced all four of what the FTC said were sound information practices. A majority of FTC commissioners said a law should be passed that would require sites to provide visitors with notice of their information policies, a choice to opt out of data collection, access to the data that have been collected about them, and top-notch security to guarantee that personal data are not stolen or leaked.

The FTC's support for such new legislation waned with the election of President George W. Bush and the subsequent rise of bigger concerns like the use of the Internet for secretly planning attacks against the United States. However, there's no guarantee that new privacy legislation will not gain support in Congress at some point in the near future.

Lawyers have told us that as long as there is no legal requirement for privacy policies, they're not terrifically enthusiastic about creating documents that can only be used against the companies that write them and then violate them.

Stephanie B. Glaser, an attorney with Patterson, Belknap, Webb & Tyler, LLP in New York City, has written on the GigaLaw.com Web site that sites that do not collect personally identifying information might not want to post a privacy policy. "Because laws mandating privacy policies are not likely to be enacted anytime soon and because owners will be strictly held to any promises or statements they may make in their policies, a decision not to post a privacy policy in these circumstances may be a rational choice," she wrote.[1]

Glaser also wrote, however, that sites that do collect personal information will probably find it worthwhile to post a privacy policy to win the cooperation of consumers who are less likely to trust a site that does not reveal what it does with personal data. "The more personal information the site collects (such as e-mail addresses, names, postal addresses, and financial information) and the more the site shares this information with third parties, the more a Web site owner should probably opt to include a privacy statement because it is simply good for business," she wrote.

Once a decision is made to post a privacy policy, the posting company is opening itself up to a potential PR disaster if it is not careful in developing its policy. Too often we've seen companies guide their policymaking by what they think people want to hear. The popular inclination is to adopt a policy

---

1. Glaser, Stephanie B., GigaLaw.com, "To Post an Online Privacy Policy Or Not?," November 2001, *gigalaw.com/articles/2001-all/glaser-2001-11-all.html.*

that portrays you or your client as a white knight with total respect for the sanctity of personal data. That's fine if you are confident that this philosophy is widely shared inside the company and your policy will not be violated the day it is posted.

We urge you to encourage your client to take the time to discuss its information practices. If there's any chance that the company might share information with a third party, you should state that in your policy and explain what those third parties might do with the data. Could you possibly be adding reporters' e-mail addresses collected for one client to an e-mail distribution list you've established for another client? Is there any chance that the newsletter e-mail list your client has created for its most loyal customers could be viewed as a saleable asset if the company folds? If your policy promises to "guarantee" the privacy of site users, do you and your client really have top-notch security measures in place to keep personal data from being hacked or accidentally made public?

A good privacy policy should describe what types of information are collected and to whom the data might be disclosed. If your site includes ads served by other companies or features managed by other service providers, you should probably point out that you are not responsible for the information practices of those other players. Another thing that many Internet users look to find in a privacy policy are details about the site's use of "cookies," a technology that can be used to track the footprints of Web site visitors in an attempt to learn their likes and dislikes. Some sites use cookies anonymously to serve up product offers they think might be of interest to a visitor without ever learning the visitor's name or other identifying information. Other sites, however, might ask users to register and will place a cookie on the user's hard drive so that the person's online footprints can be tied to his or her identifying information to keep close tabs on what a particular consumer is seeking.

If your site offers the consumer some ability to review the personal information on file or change it (i.e., the e-mail address for a newsletter), your privacy statement should say so. Consumers will also want to know whether you are using encryption or other technologies to keep their data secure. Finally, the privacy statement should also note the likelihood of future amendments to the policy and invite visitors to check back periodically.

As we noted earlier, what you put in your client's privacy policy is fantastically important because the existence of the policy opens the door for FTC review and disciplinary actions, which always amount to bad publicity for the company being investigated.

Drug company Eli Lilly learned this lesson the hard way in June 2001 when an employee sent out an e-mail message to inform users of the antidepressant Prozac that a reminder service was being discontinued. The service had been used to send regular e-mails to 669 subscribers to remind them to take their pills or refill their subscriptions. Unfortunately, the Lilly employee charged with sending the notice about the service's termination did not protect the e-mail addresses of subscribers. Consequently the addresses of fellow subscribers were visible to all recipients. The problem resulted in an FTC finding in January 2002 that the company had not kept its promise to protect the privacy of Web site visitors. The agency required Lilly to "establish and maintain a four-stage information security program designed to establish and maintain reasonable and appropriate administrative, technical, and physical safeguards to protect consumers' personal information against any reasonably anticipated threats or hazards to its security, confidentiality, or integrity, and to protect such information against unauthorized access, use, or disclosure." The company was also required to do an annual written review of its practices intended to protect privacy.[2]

The Lilly ruling is also significant for its timing because it came during the Bush Administration, signaling that the FTC would continue to police compliance with privacy policies even while arguing that a new law was not needed to require the posting of such policies. Indeed, FTC Chairman Timothy J. Muris told a House of Representatives subcommittee in April

---

2.   FTC press release, January 18, 2002.

2002 that his agency would increase its spending on efforts to oversee compliance with online privacy promises.[3]

Another thing Muris vowed to continue is the FTC's policing of the promises Web sites have made to comply with privacy regulations from the European Union (EU). The European Commission's Directive on Data Protection went into effect in October 1998, and requires companies in the 15 member nations to carefully guard the privacy of the citizens of the member countries. Given that the United States government has preferred a more hands-off approach, the directive threatened to bar many U.S. companies from doing business with citizens of EU countries. So the U.S. Commerce Department negotiated a framework with the EU under which U.S. companies can earn "safe harbor" status under the EU directive if they abide by particular information management principles. The EU lists seven principles altogether including notice, choice, access, and security, which we discussed earlier. In addition, the E.U. requires that companies provide consumers with notice and choice when their data are being transferred to a third party. The data must also be accurate and current and the company must be subject to an enforcement process if it fails to abide by its privacy statements. (For more on the safe harbor structure, see the sidebar on page 206 in this chapter.)

Once a company has drafted its privacy policy and posted it online, a certification form can be filled out on the Department of Commerce's Web site so that the company's name can be added to the safe harbor list maintained by the Commerce Department at *web.ita.doc.gov/safeharbor/shlist.nsf/webPages/ safe+harbor+list*. A company that does not abide by the policy it has adopted can be charged with deceptive practices by the FTC and could lose its safe harbor certification.

One area where the U.S. Congress has endorsed regulation on data collection is in those cases where information is collected from children under the age of 13. A 1998 law known as the Children's Online Privacy Protection Act (COPPA) prohib-

---

3.   FTC press release, April 10, 2002.

its the collection of personally identifiable information from young children without their parents' consent and the FTC has acted vigilantly to enforce the law and bring action against non-complying Web site owners. If you or your client are seeking information from Web site visitors or collecting data about newsletter subscribers, you must take steps to ensure you are not collecting data from children younger than 13 years old without the permission of their parents.

The regulations developed to implement COPPA apply to operators of commercial Web sites and online services directed to children under the age of 13, and to general-audience Web sites and online services that knowingly collect personal information from children. Among other things, the regulations require that a clear and prominent link be placed on the home page and on data-collection pages to a notice that describes a site's information practices. The notice must list the name and contact information for someone who is responsible for collecting information from children. It must also describe what types of data are collected and how they are collected—by directly asking the children or by observing their site usage through cookies or some other technology. The notice must also describe what kinds of third parties have access to the data and for what purposes. It must also advise parents of procedures to follow to review the data collected about their children.[4]

The original COPPA regulations allow site operators to obtain a parent's permission in a variety of ways, including e-mail, fax, and letter. However, those regulations have been under review and may be amended. Details about COPPA are available on the Internet at *ftc.gov/kidzprivacy.*

The FTC is responsible for policing this area and has brought cases against several Web sites alleged to have violated COPPA. In one case, the American Pop Corn Company (APC) agreed to pay $10,000 to settle FTC charges that it violated COPPA by collecting personal information from children on its

---

4.   FTC Web site document, "Facts for Businesses: How to Comply With the Children's Online Privacy Protection Rule."

"Jolly Time" Web site without obtaining parental consent. In its complaint, the FTC alleged that APC maintains a Web site at *jollytime.com* with a Kids Club section that features games, crafts, contests, and jokes directed at children under the age of 13. Without obtaining parental consent, the company collected personal information, including names, e-mail addresses, and home addresses, from children who went to the Kids Club section. It also conditioned participation in certain prize offers on children's providing more information than was necessary to participate in the activity, the FTC alleged. Both practices violate COPPA. In addition, APC posted a privacy policy statement on its Web site stating that it would notify parents or guardians by e-mail whenever "guests" under the age of 18 registered at its site. It stated that parents or guardians would be given the option to invalidate the registration. However, APC did not contact the parents of children who registered and provided personal information, and therefore the privacy policy statements were false, in violation of the FTC Act, the agency alleged.[5]

The fine was $30,000 for COPPA violations in a case the FTC brought against Lisa Frank Inc., a seller of girls' toys and school supplies that the FTC found was collecting personal information from children without their parents' consent. The agency also charged the company with deceptive practices for stating in its privacy policy that children younger than 13 would need a parent to complete the site's registration form. In fact, parents were never required to participate in the registration process.[6]

To help companies ensure that their Web sites comply with COPPA, the FTC has entered into partnerships with several "seal" programs that will review a site's policies and determine whether they comply with the law. Among the organizations the FTC has embraced are TRUSTe, an Internet privacy seal program; the Entertainment Software Rating Board; and the Children's Advertising Review Unit of the Council of Better Business Bureaus.

---

5. FTC press release, February 14, 2002.
6. FTC press release, October 2, 2001.

One other thing to be aware of when constructing a privacy policy for your firm or your clients is the emergence of a technology initiative called Platform for Privacy Preferences (P3P) that is intended to help people decide whether to visit particular Web sites depending on the contents of their privacy policies. The goal is to enable a person's browser software to automatically review privacy policies and provide access to only those sites that have policies that the users has defined as acceptable.

P3P is a standard developed by the World Wide Web Consortium. Early versions have been circulated online since 2000, but version 1.0 of P3P was issued as a recommendation in April 2002. FTC Chairman Muris gave the effort his endorsement in October 2001 when he told the Privacy 2001 Conference that it was "cutting-edge technology" that represented an approach to handling privacy concerns that is "much more manageable than today's site-by-site, notice-by-notice regime."[7]

P3P works by requiring a site to boil its privacy policy down to a series of answers to a set of multiple choice questions. An Internet user, armed with a P3P-compliant browser, such as Microsoft Internet Explorer 6, must complete a similar questionnaire to specify what he or she considers to be acceptable privacy policies. The technology then notifies a visitor of the acceptability of a site's policies when he or she enters the site or moves to different pages within a site. A user, for example, might specify that she does not want her e-mail address shared with a site's marketing partners. A site that intends to share e-mail addresses with third parties will be flagged by the user's browser software, thus notifying the user of the need to cancel her transaction or opt out of this site's data sharing activities.

Because any Web page with a URL can have its own P3P policy, we recommend that you conduct an audit of your site to determine what types of data are being collected on each page and for what purposes. Different policies can then be

---

7.   FTC press release, October 4, 2001.

associated with each page, thereby enabling you to disclose, for example, that data entered on contest forms are shared with third parties, whereas data entered on the site registration page are not shared outside your company. The actual machine-readable privacy policies are created using generator software available through *p3ptoolbox.org*.

Although the list of sites complying with P3P is still relatively short in comparison to the size of the Internet, it continues to grow and many Internet analysts believe the technology could be an important means by which people become more comfortable with how their personal data are used online.

SIDEBAR:
UNDERSTANDING THE EU SAFE HARBOR AGREEMENT

The U.S. Commerce Department has published the following questions and answers related to the safe harbor agreement that enables self-certified U.S. companies to do business with citizens of EU nations. The following is excerpted from a longer list of questions and answers on the department's Web site at *export.gov/safeharbor/sh_overview.html*.

What do the safe harbor principles require?

Organizations must comply with the seven safe harbor principles. The principles require the following:

Notice: Organizations must notify individuals about the purposes for which they collect and use information about them. They must provide information about how individuals can contact the organization with any inquiries or complaints, the types of third parties to which it discloses the information and the choices and means the organization offers for limiting its use and disclosure.

Choice: Organizations must give individuals the opportunity to choose (opt out) whether their personal information will be disclosed to a third party or used for a purpose incompatible with the purpose for which it was originally collected or subsequently authorized by the individual. For sensitive information, affirmative or explicit (opt in) choice must be given if the information is to be disclosed to a third party or used for a purpose other than its original purpose or the purpose authorized subsequently by the individual.

Onward Transfer (Transfers to Third Parties): To disclose information to a third party, organizations must apply the notice and choice principles. Where an organization wishes to transfer information to a third party that is acting as an agent, it may do so if it makes sure that the third party subscribes to the safe harbor principles or is subject to the Directive or another adequacy finding. As an alternative, the organization can enter into a written agreement with such third party requiring that the third party provide at least the same level of privacy protection as is required by the relevant principles.

Access: Individuals must have access to personal information about them that an organization holds and be able to correct, amend, or delete that information where it is inaccurate, except where the burden or expense of providing access would be disproportionate to the risks to the individual's privacy in the case in question, or where the rights of persons other than the individual would be violated.

Security: Organizations must take reasonable precautions to protect personal information from loss, misuse, and unauthorized access, disclosure, alteration, and destruction.

Data Integrity: Personal information must be relevant for the purposes for which it is to be used. An organization should take reasonable steps to ensure that data is reliable for its intended use, accurate, complete, and current.

Enforcement: In order to ensure compliance with the safe harbor principles, there must be (a) readily available and affordable independent recourse mechanisms so that each individual's complaints and disputes can be investigated and resolved and damages awarded where the applicable law or private sector initiatives so provide; (b) procedures for verifying that the commitments companies make to adhere to the safe harbor principles have been implemented; and (c) obligations to remedy problems arising out of a failure to comply with the principles. Sanctions must be sufficiently rigorous to ensure compliance by the organization. Organizations that fail to provide annual self-certification letters will no longer appear in the list of participants and safe harbor benefits will no longer be assured.

How and where will the safe harbor be enforced?

In general, enforcement of the safe harbor will take place in the United States in accordance with U.S. law and will be carried out primarily by the private sector. Private sector self-regulation and enforcement will be backed up as needed by government enforcement of the federal and state unfair and deceptive statutes. The intent of these statutes is to give an organization's safe harbor commitments the force of law vis-à-vis that organization. ∎

IV CONCLUSIONS

14 THE CHANGING ROLE OF THE COMMUNICATOR

➤ The Internet revolution promises profound changes in public relations.
➤ The PR professional is empowered to play a more important role in crafting a client's message and image.
➤ Our tools and vocabulary have been changed forever.

"Revolutionize" is a word that was thrown around with reckless abandon during the heyday of Internet startups. The Internet was going to revolutionize how we shopped for everything from soft drinks to sofas to SUVs. It was going to revolutionize how we booked plane trips and hotel rooms. It was going to revolutionize the concept of community by creating virtual communities of like-minded individuals regardless of geographic distance. The Internet was going to revolutionize relationships between manufacturers and suppliers.

As we look back on it, some of these revolutions have achieved more than others. However, we think it is appropriate to use the word "revolutionize" to explain what the Internet has done to public relations.

The revolution is reflected in the new tools like e-mail, online pressrooms, newsletters, and Webcasts that we've devoted large portions of this book to discussing. At the heart of this revolution, though, is a profound change in the role of the public relations professional. What the Internet has done is freed the public relations professional to be less of a paper shuffler and more of a thinker. In short, it lets you work smarter.

Frequently, it is the technology itself that is characterized as "smart." We have smart bombs that allow the military to locate precise targets and we have smart houses that turn on the lawn sprinkler and close the window blinds when the sun emerges from behind a cloud on a hot summer day. However, technology developers will tell you that a technology is not really pulling its weight until it enables humans to work more efficiently and effectively.

In public relations, this brass ring is now within reach. PR professionals who are taking advantage of the Internet to keep their media lists updated and to get their press releases distributed via e-mail and archived in an online pressroom are finding themselves spending less time on faxing and overnight mail and misdirected pitches to inappropriate media outlets. Instead, they have time to think more strategically about the message that their clients are delivering—online and offline—and how the media and the public are responding. They are evolving beyond the role of "contact person" to a fuller partnership with marketing people, IT departments, and top executives in crafting the image of the company or organization.

This theme has been raised by several professionals—from both the PR side and the journalism side—in their comments throughout this book.

Larry Weber, chairman and CEO of Interpublic's Advanced Marketing Services, says that the evolution of PR people from distributors of information to strategists promises to change the makeup of the PR industry. The people needed for such jobs are more likely to be the types of students who historically have tended to pursue MBAs or law degrees rather than going into public relations, Weber says. This means that salaries in PR might have to rise to reel in the best and the brightest, he acknowledges, but so should the quality of the service being provided to the clients.

Matthew Anchin of IBM, who manages that company's online pressroom, also talked to us about the new PR skill set. With the Internet playing such an important role in distributing information, it becomes more important for PR people to be able to explain a company's business strategy, including how a new product fits in with that strategy and how it compares to those of industry rivals, Anchin says. In the case of IBM, he says, it is very likely that more of the company's PR people will be hired with non-traditional PR backgrounds. For instance, someone with an engineering degree could speak intelligently about the company's vision and its products.

For Dianne Lynch, a journalism professor at St. Michael's College, the Internet forces PR people to evolve to remain "relevant," because they no longer serve the role of information gateway. With so much data available online, a reporter is not beholden to a PR person for a copy of the latest releases or the annual report, says Lynch in Chapter 6, pointing out that online directories often enable reporters to directly dial a company's executives without the aid of PR people. She also sees PR people playing a larger role as strategists helping to keep a client's public messages in line with its business goals and she suggests that PR professionals should also help coach top executives to keep them on-message when speaking publicly.

Whether or not you're ready to agree that the Internet promises to redefine the PR profession, you cannot deny that it has already changed the day-to-day activities of PR professionals.

Take a moment to consider where you were 10 years ago. Were you in school, in business, or perhaps one of the first to realize that this new application called the World Wide Web was going to someday affect the entire scope of your day? The world is a much smaller and faster place than it was a decade ago. Change is a constant and the word "constant" barely exists.

Think about a few of the major milestones since you first realized that you could work more quickly and collaboratively via e-mail with a client in another time zone or hemisphere. You also learned that e-mail got your message to the media more quickly than typing letters, printing them out, and addressing a couple of hundred envelopes. What about the ability you were given to generate an accurate media list with a few simple strokes on a keyboard? Before online media guides came along, it might have taken a dozen phone calls to get the name of the right editor to whom to send a press kit or a news release. What a tremendous difference to have a vendor (i.e., Bacon's or Media Map) update the online database daily.

The Web gives you a greater ability to find out who's writing about your clients and why. Monitoring services like CyberAlert and eWatch tell you about not only the traditional media, but about rumor mongers who might be planning to tarnish your client's reputation.

Another way to consider how far we've come in 10 years is to consider the things that you worry about today that you didn't even know about in the early 1990s. We submit the following list of new worries:

- The Internet forces PR professionals to learn more about technology and to communicate more closely with internal IT departments or the IT departments of their clients. Today's PR professional must have a vocabulary that includes many technological terms.
- The Internet forces PR professionals to understand the importance of Web site design and how a consistent look and feel for a brand is important to its online presence.
- The Internet keeps your clients "in play" 24 hours a day, 7 days a week, because information is always available on the Web to reporters in any number of countries and individuals are always free to launch new message boards or Web sites that cast your client in a negative light.

Perhaps the simplest way to recognize how the Internet has changed you in the last 10 years is to listen to yourself talk. If you're like many of us, you're probably surprised by the number of technical terms that roll off your tongue that were known by a small number of technophiles at the beginning of the 1990s. Take a look at "The New PR Glossary" we've assembled in this chapter (see page 216) and see how many you already know.

What's remarkable is the extent to which today's PR professionals encounter the terminology all the time. Consider the example of a young PR professional who knows just what she needs to do when she gets a call from a frenzied photo editor on deadline who wants a color image of her client and adds: "Make sure it's 300 dpi." That same young colleague also does not miss a beat when she must explain to a client that he can see draft versions of news releases and media kit designs on her PR firm's staging server. When the client asks, "What's a staging server?" today's PR professional knows what to tell him.

The pace of technological change is certainly not going to slow down, not even with a slowdown in capital spending that is delaying moves to broadband, and other technologies. We'll offer some thoughts on what the future might hold in our next chapter. As we wrap up this chapter, however, we'll predict that it will continue to be up to PR professionals to listen, to learn, and to be open to new technological advances that affect the PR profession—all in an effort to better serve a client and a brand. PR professionals cannot stop at any point and say "I've learned enough today." The nature of the profession promotes continuous learning, and we believe this must include information technology. We feel the changes and the challenges prepare you to be proactive and responsive with your clients' or your company's PR needs.

Remember, this changing role that you're experiencing is really just one more constant that you can count on day in and day out. After all, as you change and hone your Internet and PR skills, more and more opportunities will become available to those you serve. And, as you change and grow with technology, you help to shape the future direction of the public relations industry and the Internet. In reality, it's your toolkit and you're building it every step of the way.

SIDEBAR: THE NEW PR GLOSSARY

It's remarkable to consider how much technology jargon has crept into the everyday vocabulary of PR people who are working with the Internet. Test yourself to see how many of the terms on our list you already know:

- **Archive:** Older files that are no longer timely, but are still available to users who might be interested.

- **Back-end programming:** Any programming or code that helps build the site but remains invisible to the user.

- **Bandwidth:** The amount of information that can be sent through a network connection at one time, usually measured in bits per second (bps). The larger a file, image, or video, the longer it will take, especially over low-bandwidth connections.

- **Domain name:** The name that people will use to visit a site (e.g., *yourcompany.com*).

- **Firewall:** The hardware and software used to break up a network into one or more parts for security reasons. Firewalls keep some Internet users from accessing some Internet features, such as Webcasts.

- **Front-end design:** The graphic designs, text, logos, and all of the elements that are seen on a Web site.

- **FTP:** File Transfer Protocol, which provides the ability to move files between two Internet sites. You'll often hear IT people saying (although considered slang to some), "Please FTP that over to them," or "I already FTPed that."

- **Hits:** Requests made of the Web server to relay a file back to the user, hence the phrase, "How many hits has this page received?"

- **HTML:** Hypertext Markup Language. Don't let the acronym scare you. It's a simple coding language that tells a Web browser how to lay out elements on each Web page.

- **IP address:** A numeric address to determine where a Web site resides on the Internet. Your domain name has a numeric equivalent that might look something like 67.80.99.34

- **ISP:** Internet Service Provider. These are the companies that help connect us and provide access to the World Wide Web.

- **JPEG:** A file format used to share images over the Web (the other popular format is a GIF). JPEGs tend to show colors and photographic images better, and therefore are more desired by editors for print publications. Editors will usually covert JPEGs into TIFFs, which are among the more popular print formats.

- **Server:** A computer where the files needed to create a Web site reside. When a user looks for a Web site, he or she is sending a message to the server, which then displays the necessary files.

- **Staging server:** A computer that is used to display files or work before it's published on the Web. Companies use these staging servers internally to allow clients or company executives to preview work prior to it going live on a Web site.

- **300 dpi:** 300 dots per inch is considered a high-resolution image. The more dots per inch, the better the resolution and clarity of the image. Editors tend to ask for 300 dpi images that they can download from the Web and then use for their print articles. Additionally, many Web graphics (not meant for print) are created at 72 dpi.

- **Unique users:** A calculation of the number of users to a site that avoids the recounting of repeat visitors.

- **URL:** Uniform Resource Locator; an address for a source on the Internet. When you type *http://www.thesitesname.com*, you are typing a URL.

- **Web browser:** The program that allows people to view the Web. Internet Explorer and Netscape Navigator are popular examples.

- **Web log:** A record of demographic information about the visitors that come to a site, including geography, paths through the site, and so on.

- **Video on demand:** Video that is recorded to tape and then stored on the Internet to be viewed by users at any time. Although the video was taped at an earlier point in time, the users can view the video on the Internet at their convenience. ■

PR REFLECTIONS: TOM NOLAN OF PUBLICIS DIALOG

We asked Tom Nolan, a management supervisor for the public relations division of Publicis Dialog for his reflections on the changing role of the communicator. Tom has more than nine years of technology, business-to-business, and health-care public relations experience. He has managed publicity campaigns and served as lead media placement specialist for several Fortune 500 corporations.

I'm approaching my tenth year in the public relations industry, putting me right in the middle of the job experience pack—not yet the level of long-term veteran, but far from a "wet behind the ears" rookie. However, I joined the industry just as it was starting to undergo a massive change and I was able to experience firsthand the tremendous growth of PR over the last decade, putting us where we are today.

The 90s PR wave saw new firms sprouting up all over the country and in-house corporate communications staffs increasing. Salaries started to rise and experts in PR niche areas (such as new media and crisis communications) were being sought out. For myself, the most revealing thing was the reduction in peculiar "explain to me again what you do for a living" looks I was receiving from my wife and family members.

The biggest change, of course, came from the expansion of the Internet—it not only changed how to approach PR strategies, but it dramatically increased the number of media outlets to target. Public relations and the Internet are a perfect match, as the initial idea of the World Wide Web was to create a place to find information and the idea of public relations is to supply information. In fact, as the Internet evolved, so did public relations.

Despite all the changes and growth over the last 10 years, at its core, public relations is the same today as it was when I took my first entry-level job. The basic concept is still to spread the word about an idea, company, person, etc., through ongoing media activities designed to generate press coverage. The tactics may change, but the objectives are still the same.

The opportunity for press coverage is greater than ever today because of the increased number of media outlets. However one of the issues public relations professionals must still contend with is a client who wants a big media placement, and feels the best way to do it is to bombard the press with meaningless company news. The throw-everything-against-the-wall-and-hope-something-sticks theory is simply bad PR. Not everything is newsworthy and every company activity does not need a press release. The deluge of unimportant news items has created tension between PR pros and the press.

Most of my success with the media has come from only pitching items that have some news value. Additionally, offering exclusives (reporters love that—the last thing they want to see is their story in four other publications) and being familiar with the magazine and the reporter's work are also essential. The idea is to work with the press, not against them.

A perfect example of bad PR was during the dot-com rage. As I said, the Internet changed the PR industry, but both received deserved black eyes during the late 90s dot-com boom and subsequent bust. It seemed every startup Internet company was paying a public relations agency to promote their products and new business models, in order to secure millions in seed investments. When it became evident to the media that the majority of these companies had nothing to show but "vaporware," the backlash began. Hopefully the industry has learned its lesson in the post–dot-com era.

It's an interesting environment in today's PR world and I know the profession will continue to grow, simply because people will continue to read. TV will continue to be watched. The Web will continue to be surfed. It's been an exciting 10 years and I can't wait to see what the next decade has in store. ■

We asked Ed Emerman, president of Eagle Public Relations in Princeton, New Jersey, for his reflections on the changing role of the communicator. With more than 20 years of experience in human resources, insurance, and health-care PR, Ed touched on some key issues with change and the media in this essay that he's titled, "Technology & Communication with the Media."

Without question, technology has had more impact on the public relations industry than any other development in the 20 years that I've been involved in this business. And for the most part, technological advancements have enabled public relations professionals to do their jobs more efficiently.

Take, for example, how technology has changed the way we communicate with the media. I can recall back in the 1980s, having a team of PR professionals manually stuffing news releases into envelopes, handwriting personal notes to each one, and then bringing them to the mailroom to send out. Critical media might be fortunate enough to have a messenger personally deliver the release to them. Fax machines ultimately improved the process, but even that method of transmitting releases has become a dinosaur thanks to e-mail and the use of electronic distribution services.

But this technology has also created headaches, or should I say challenges, too. Some reporters still insist on receiving press releases via snail mail. Others want them faxed into the newsroom. Send a release by e-mail to certain reporters and it's likely to be greeted with the delete button. Other reporters who accept e-mail insist on news releases that are pasted into an e-mail message rather than sent as an attachment. The end result? PR pros need to keep tabs on how to best communicate with reporters . . . easier said than done. ■

15 Looking Ahead

> ➤ Technology tears down walls and aids collaboration.
> ➤ New tools like instant messaging and wireless devices have PR potential.
> ➤ 3D graphics promise help in explaining complex topics.
> ➤ Management software aims to make PR firms smarter and answer calls for accountability.

What comes after the Internet? If you accept our premise that the Internet has changed public relations—and the entire business world—forever, then the natural question is, "What comes next?"

If we were any good at forecasting technology trends, we'd probably have become rich investors a long time ago and retired from the public relations and journalism businesses. Obviously, no one can say with any certainty what new tools PR professionals can expect to integrate into their strategies in the next three to five years, but it's always fun to speculate.

What follows are some things that we think are worth watching, plus some suggestions we received from academics and PR practitioners.

MORE COLLABORATION

One popular prediction is that physical barriers between PR people and their clients and between PR people and journalists will continue to be surmounted with technology. Several PR people told us that networks—often called extranets—that link together PR firms and their clients would grow in popularity. They said they anticipated greater use of collaborative technology that enables a PR person and a client to work on the draft of a press release together. Such applications allow a PR person in New York to write a draft and the client in Missouri to edit the document immediately. Jennifer Guberman, director of information services for Magnet Communications in New York, told us that the demand for extranets and collaboration cannot be ignored because it is coming from clients. "Clients really want that ability to collaborate," she said. "Clients are expecting more access and interaction than they did previously."

Journalists and PR people aren't going to be editing documents together in the future, but several PR professionals told us that they expected greater use of Internet conferencing technologies like WebEx or PlaceWare that enable people to meet over the Internet. Audio and video of the two parties can be supplemented with PowerPoint slides and other materials that help the PR person and the client explain their product or service offering. As we noted in Chapter 9, videoconferencing over the Internet has picked up momentum because of improving technology and the declining economy of the new millennium, which have caused many PR clients and media organizations to cut back on travel expenses.

Another tool that brings parties together and aids collaboration is instant messaging. We noted in Chapter 2 that it is extremely popular among young people who might bring it with them to the business world in the near future. What we've heard from a few PR practitioners is that instant messaging is already being used as a way to handle quick questions between colleagues in remote locations and between PR firms and their clients, furthering strengthening the collaborative bond. Few

PR professionals said they anticipated instant messages becoming a popular means of communicating with journalists. Most told us they expected journalists to be unwilling to share their IM addresses with them and we tend to agree that few, if any, journalists we know would be willing to accept instant messages from PR people.

However, Rory J. O'Connor, vice president for strategic communications at Dittus Communications in Washington, DC, is a former journalist who thinks PR professionals could develop instant messaging services for which reporters would sign up. He suggests, as an example, that a company that is the subject of a Congressional hearing might offer an instant messaging service to reporters that enabled them to get the company's responses to Congressional allegations on their cell phones and PDAs while they are still sitting at the press table in the hearing room. Reporters might also be able to ask questions of the company's PR team via instant messaging, O'Connor suggests.

O'Connor's example points up another emerging trend cited by several PR practitioners, which is the growth in the use of handheld devices connected to the Internet. Several PR people point out that the devices have tremendous value internally as a means by which traveling PR reps can remain connected to e-mail. They can also be used to get information to a client's CEO who has consented to do an interview while on the road. Instant messaging can also be used during the interview to remind the executive of important points to make.

Reporters are also using the devices as a means of doing research when they are away from their offices. Magnet's Guberman says her firm is responding to this development by encouraging clients to offer text-only versions of the documents on its Web site that can be transferred and displayed on a small device much more easily than can regular Web pages laden with images, animation, and other features. She notes that offering the text-only option is also appreciated by PC owners who still have slow dial-up connections to the Internet and by visually impaired people who rely on text-reading software to use the Internet. "You do want to reach the most people," Guberman notes.

RICHER PRESENTATIONS

At the same time, however, many other PR professionals tell us that technology is pulling them in the other direction—away from text and toward richer information services. Press releases with images and video are already becoming more popular and that trend will surely continue. Steve Capoccia, general manager of Lewis PR in Newton, Massachusetts, told us that creating videos is so easy and inexpensive that it has to catch on. His firm uses a Sony camcorder and a Macintosh computer running iMovie software to create quick, introductory video clips that can be shared online with prospective clients and journalists. He says improvements in compression technology are eliminating the jerky pictures that turned some people against online video in the past. The last hurdle for many people, he says, will be getting comfortable with being on camera and not worrying about their appearance or where they should be looking. "People are afraid of video because they don't know how to behave with it," Capoccia says.

Other practitioners, such as Magnet's Guberman, go beyond video in their visions of future press releases. She says that improving bandwidth and the ever-increasing processor speeds on PCs will make it possible in the next two years for PR people to include 3D demonstrations in a client's online pressroom or as an attachment to a press release. She notes that iPIX imaging technology already enables Web users to take "virtual tours" of some restaurants and resorts and virtual reality software is used to enable an Internet user to feel like he or she is walking through a museum and handling artifacts.

O'Connor of Dittus Communications agrees that virtual reality software packages like QuickTime VR promise to help PR people communicate more effectively. He suggests, for example, that a 3D simulation of a blowout would be great to support a safety campaign for a tire manufacturer that urges consumers to keep their tires properly inflated. "There's all kinds of new possibilities," he says.

Professor James S. O'Rourke, IV, of the Mendoza College of Business at the University of Notre Dame, says PR people should be thinking of how to communicate effectively with people who learn in different ways. "If you can't say it to them, you may be able to show it to them," he says, noting that research has found that some people learn best by seeing or hearing rather than through reading.

O'Rourke says some of the technology that could help PR people create visualizations might be right under our noses. "Look at the gaming business," he says. "That's becoming more and more sophisticated."

BLOGS ARE COMING

We noted in Chapter 10 that the Internet is always capable of sprouting new discussion groups or bulletin boards where your client might find itself bloodied or praised. Laura Goldberg of Trylon Communications in New York predicts the growth of Weblogs—often referred to as *blogs*—that feature discussions of the latest news in a particular area of interest. In an August 2002 article for *PRSA Tactics Magazine,* she and colleague Lloyd Trufelman referred to Slashdot (*slashdot.org*) as an influential technology blog and to a pop-culture blog called Plastic (*plastic.com*). They recommended that PR people tread carefully in such forums, which have not traditionally been welcoming to commercial interests. A traditional pitch letter might not be appropriate, they wrote, but it might be okay to make a blog owner aware of links to some media coverage your client has received. Trufelman and Goldberg noted that blog owners tend to read each other's blogs, so a mention on one blog can be picked up on others and help get your message out.

Drew Peloso, meanwhile, thinks blogs are most valuable to PR people as knowledge-capturing forums that the PR people can create on their own. Peloso, CEO of Onclave Inc. in Princeton, New Jersey, is developing software for PR professionals that would equip them to set up blogs for their clients. He says blogs might be particularly helpful as a crisis management tool because they can be updated regularly and provide people with an opportunity to post their own comments. The goal, he notes, is to create a place where people feel comfortable contributing information and where they see the host company as a trusted source of reliable information, which they don't have to go out and collect on their own. "What people appreciate more than anything on the Internet is someone saving them time," says Peloso.

He also suggests that blogs could be used as communications tools between PR firms and their clients. People on both sides of the relationship would participate in a blog that reports on a particular topic of interest and could share their impressions and expertise with each other, Peloso says.

Another innovation that could affect public relations professionals is the concept of personalized newspapers. Walter Bender is a professor in the MIT Media Lab who is studying the idea of creating newspapers that are tailored to the interests of the reader and deliver relevant articles from publishers all across the Internet. This concept of the "Daily Me," as Bender calls it, has ramifications for PR practitioners, who would be wise to figure out how to become contributors of articles that would be delivered directly to consumers with a high degree of interest in a particular topic. We must interject that although we find personalized newspapers to be an attractive idea, we've yet to see a viable business model attached to such efforts. Advertising is not going to carry the day and successful subscription-based efforts online are still quite rare.

BETTER MANAGEMENT

Another area where we see technological advancements of value to public relations is in software intended to help PR people do their jobs better. Magnet's Guberman points out that many PR firms would benefit from knowing more about what their employees know. She says she expects to see knowledge management software used to keep track of the work history of a PR firm's employees, a practice Magnet has already adopted. These data can be used in assigning employees to various projects so that they are chosen based on their familiarity with an industry or their knowledge of a client or its competitors, she says.

Although smarter use of human resources is a goal worth pursuing, there is probably even more to be gained by turning to technology to automate so much of the record keeping that PR people do. With clients so eager in recent years to calculate the ROI for their PR dollars, technology that provides PR firms with an automated way to keep track of their contacts with reporters is in the works.

Peter Granat, senior vice president of MediaMap, told us in 2002 that his company was developing a suite of applications that would help PR people keep track of their contacts with reporters—on the phone, through the mail, or across the Internet—and assess the outcomes of those contacts. He likened the software to customer relationship management software that is used by many companies to track every contact they have with a customer, whether it's on the Web, in person, or through a customer service phone call.

"PR is one of the most relationship-intensive businesses," Granat said. "We're looking at capturing as many of those interactions with the media as possible." He says interactions could be captured when a PR person makes a record of a phone call or a fax transmission or when the PR firm's computers e-mail a press release to a reporter. Granat acknowledges that reporters' footprints are hard to track in most online pressrooms where visitors remain anonymous, but he suggests that the growing popularity of targeted opt-in newsletters will allow a PR firm to know what has been delivered to a reporter.

MediaMap aims to supplement this library of contacts with monitoring activities in partnership with Factiva that are aimed at assessing what is written or broadcast about a client, Granat said. Having an assessment of all the inputs (contacts) and outputs (clippings) should enable users of MediaMap's software to calculate the frequently requested ROI figures.

O'Connor of Dittus sees another opportunity to help PR people do their jobs better in potential software products for creating media lists. He anticipates that vendors will soon create software that lets a PR person take an electronic listing from a media directory and easily annotate it with his or her own comments about the reporter's publication and personal preferences. Ideally, O'Connor says, the software would help a PR professional target the list by removing the names of reporters who do not respond in some way to earlier mailings.

A final anticipated innovation comes in the area of search technology, where research is being done on better ways to find what an Internet user is looking for without all the useless material that often ends up in a list of search results. Many technology researchers talk about the emergence of smart software agents that a user would instruct to go across the Internet in search of particular bits of information. Dennis Chominsky at PFS Marketwyse says smarter searching would benefit PR people in their research on prospective clients, clients' competitors, journalists, and so forth. "There is still a ton of information that hasn't made it's way on to the Internet," he points out. "When and if it's ever possible to get that information online, the need for advanced search features and programmable agents will be even more valuable than we realize today."

A TOOL IS A TOOL

As we bring this book to a close, it probably provides no comfort to the reader to recognize that the tremendous changes the Internet has brought to public relations are likely to continue as technologists come up with ways to help us work smarter and more efficiently. Indeed, it seems as if there is never time to catch one's breath before we're running to catch up with the latest innovation.

As Magnet's Guberman told us, clients are now a lot more technology savvy and will be demanding that PR firms provide them with the best tools for their campaigns. At the same time it is important to remember the principle with which we started this book: No technology can replace a smart public relations strategist and a poor strategist cannot hide behind the technology for too long.

The Internet enables you to get your client's message out quickly and to make it accessible around the globe 24 hours a day and seven days a week. The Internet in many ways takes over the distribution role filled by PR professionals in the past. However, the more important strategy-making role is still reserved for the humans, and it is now more important than ever that the strategy you develop is properly executed in every press release, every Web site feature, and every e-mailed correspondence. Those strategies need to be solid, just as they were in the days of typewriters and telegrams.

All the technology in the world is not going to save a PR campaign that is fundamentally flawed. You still need a story that is worth telling, a list of media contacts that is carefully researched, and an attention-grabbing hook that no computer could ever generate.

INDEX

8 reasons why you should read the Financial Times for 4 weeks RISK-FREE!

To help you stay current with significant
developments in the world economy ...
and to assist you to make informed business
decisions — the Financial Times brings you:

❶ Fast, meaningful overviews of international affairs ... plus daily briefings on major world news.

❷ Perceptive coverage of economic, business, financial and political developments with special focus on emerging markets.

❸ More international business news than any other publication.

❹ Sophisticated financial analysis and commentary on world market activity plus stock quotes from over 30 countries.

❺ Reports on international companies and a section on global investing.

❻ Specialized pages on management, marketing, advertising and technological innovations from all parts of the world.

❼ Highly valued single-topic special reports (over 200 annually) on countries, industries, investment opportunities, technology and more.

❽ The Saturday Weekend FT section — a globetrotter's guide to leisure-time activities around the world: the arts, fine dining, travel, sports and more.

FT FINANCIAL TIMES
World business newspaper

The *Financial Times* delivers a world of business news.

Use the Risk-Free Trial Voucher below!

To stay ahead in today's business world you need to be well-informed on a daily basis. And not just on the national level. You need a news source that closely monitors the entire world of business, and then delivers it in a concise, quick-read format.

With the *Financial Times* you get the major stories from every region of the world. Reports found nowhere else. You get business, management, politics, economics, technology and more.

Now you can try the *Financial Times* for 4 weeks, absolutely risk free. And better yet, if you wish to continue receiving the *Financial Times* you'll get great savings off the regular subscription rate. Just use the voucher below.

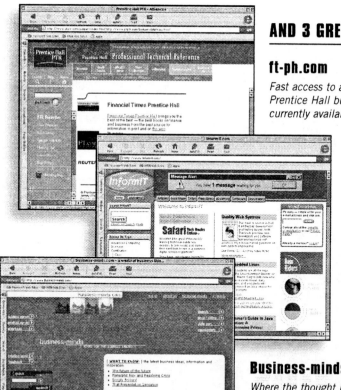